A New Monastic Handbook

A New Monastic Handbook

From Vision to Practice

Ian Mobsby and Mark Berry

CANTERBURY
PRESS
Norwich

© Ian Mobsby and Mark Berry

Published in 2014 by Canterbury Press

Editorial office
3rd Floor
Invicta House
108–114 Golden Lane,
London
EC1Y 0TG

Canterbury Press is an imprint of Hymns Ancient & Modern Ltd
(a registered charity)
13A Hellesdon Park Road
Norwich NR6 5DR, UK

www.canterburypress.co.uk

British Library Cataloguing in Publication data

A catalogue record for this book is available
from the British Library

978 1 84825 458 9

Typeset by Regent Typesetting
Printed and bound by
Ashford Colour Press Ltd

Contents

Introduction

The restoration of the church will surely come only from a new kind of Monasticism which will have nothing in common with the old but a life of uncompromising adherence to the Sermon on the Mount in imitation of Christ.

Dietrich Bonhoeffer[1]

We live in an extraordinary time in the Western world, when church attendances are diminishing but spiritual hunger is rising.

Dave Tomlinson[2]

New monastic Christians do not walk around town in black or brown robes. Yet a monastic spirituality and sensibility informs our identity. Some of us have stated solemn intentions to our bishop, to one another, and to a 'rhythm of life' (what the ancients called a 'rule'). We made our decision to walk this way not only for ourselves, but together and for others. We believe that in the midst of a culture whose primary commitment is to the self and consumerism, monasticism has something to offer ourselves, the rising numbers of the 'spiritually curious' and the many for whom life is painful and lacking in meaning about the project of being and becoming more human. And so, in our everyday clothes, we make these commitments to one another, to our church, and to living an ancient way of life in a radically different context.

Today, the Church and the Christian faith face a major cultural change. Many parts of the post-industrial Western world are increasingly post-church (a culture where the majority of the

---

1 Dietrich Bonhoeffer, from a letter to Karl-Friedrich Bonhoeffer, 1935.
2 Dave Tomlinson, 2009, *Re-Enchanting Christianity: Faith in an Emerging Culture*, Norwich: Canterbury Press, p. x.

population do not attend church and no longer see the Church as a major feature of life), post-Christian (a culture which was once predominantly Christian and had values determined by the teaching of the Church but is now multi-faith and multicultural), post-secular (a culture which had seen religion and spirituality as dead and of no relevance but is now beginning to rediscover their value), post-Christendom (a culture in which Christianity had held significant power and influence but now does not) and post-modern (a cultural reaction to the assumed certainty of scientific, or objective, efforts to explain reality). 'Spiritual, not religious' is the fastest growing religious identification.[3] People are seeking new solutions to the spiritual and existential questions they face, and many are not finding answers in traditional churches. This is not all negative. The fact that people are seeking spirituality in an increasingly post-secular culture is an opportunity for the Church to respond in innovative mission, to build new and authentic forms of church.

The shift going on in our postmodern and post-secular context is not so different from the changes faced by Anthony and his companions in the third century as they set out to found monasticism in the deserts of Egypt and Syria. From its beginnings, the Church had comprised a group of societal outsiders, living a radically different life from the excesses and power abuses of the Roman Empire. As Christianity became accepted as the authorized religion under Emperor Constantine, the Church was radically reorientated by a change in its nature into what has sometimes been called 'Christendom'. By becoming the official mainstream religion, the Church became part of the establishment absorbing the values of political power, money, patriarchal hierarchy and a focus on the rich and influential rather than the poor and marginalized. The early desert mothers and fathers felt that something was being lost and responded by seeking to retain something of the previous DNA of Christianity and the Church by going into the deserts. The first rules or rhythms of life were a reaction against Christendom. Poverty as a response to increased power and materialism, obedience in response to individualism,

---

3 http://pewforum.org/Age/Religion-Among-the-Millennials.aspx.

hedonism and the Emperor Cult (because Jesus was God not the Emperor) and chastity in response to sexual promiscuity and licentiousness.

Much is now written about new monasticism in the USA, in the UK and around the world. This growing library has emphasized the call for action outside the bubble of comfortable Sunday worship services by going to serve God in many different areas of our own communities. There is much poverty and impoverishment in contemporary culture that has created a hunger and yearning for mysticism and spirituality which is practical and accessible to ordinary people. This is, at its heart, a reopening of Christian spirituality and formation through the call to mission and, more precisely, the loving intentions of God who seeks for all things to be restored into right relationship with the Holy Trinity. This is the core practice to which monastics (who gravitate to places of prayer, service and withdrawal from general life) and mendicants (friars who were called to serve God in small missional communities to particular places where the Church was weak) have given obedience: to love God, love yourself and love others.

This book is written out of our shared conviction that new monasticism is inspired by a particular understanding of God the Trinity (the nature of God, God as holy community, God one yet three, God as unity in diversity), that has much to say about what church is. As God is a dynamic event of grace where the Three Persons of God practise perfect unity, love, justice, equality and inclusion, so the Church is called to be an imperfect representative community of the one perfect divine community of God.

New monasticism is not about a romantic withdrawal to beautiful and privileged places in the countryside, fleeing from the problems of the world, but rather a radical commitment to stay with and re-engage in mission, seeking the kingdom of God in places where God can feel absent. We have many friends throughout the world where there is either a deep spiritual hunger for meaning and belonging or a desire for hope and the alleviation of pain, hopelessness and suffering while rejecting mainstream Christianity. So who is going to engage with the many people who are spiritually curious and hungry for transformation and

liberation, seeking alternatives to the dehumanizing effects of
the global market and what has become known as 'ecocide': the
combination of global warming, deforestation and reducing bio-
diversity? What forms of church are going to assist such people
who do not trust church and religion to experience Jesus Christ?
Who is going to help such people to become Christian pilgrims?
We hope this book will help some to engage in this journey.

So what do we mean by a new monastic community? This book
is an attempt to answer this important question. We believe that
the distinctiveness of a new monastic community is the combination of a number of features. None of these features are unique
to new monasticism, but it is the particular combination of these
features that defines the essence of what new monasticism seeks
to be. These features are explored in detail:

1. A formal written rhythm of life that includes seasonal aspirations, spiritual practices and postures (Chapters 4 and 5)
2. A commitment to being missional and contextual (Chapter 7)
3. A variant vocation to being a new monastic 'monk', 'monk-
   friar' or 'friar'[4] (Chapter 10)
4. A commitment to participative governance (Chapter 11)
5. Worship that is participative, contemplative and sacramental
   (Chapter 6)
6. A commitment to non-dualism and non-tribalism (Chapter 8)
7. A commitment to post-Christendom and servant discipleship
   (Chapter 8)
8. Deeply Trinitarian in belief and practice (Chapter 3)
9. Experimental and creative in spirit and practice (Chapter 6)
10. Radical yet fully integrated into the local church (Chapter 8)
11. Fluid at the edges yet deeply centred (Chapter 11)
12. Flexible and relational by being small and missional (Chapter
    10)
13. Offering 'whole-of-life', incarnational and experiential
    approaches to Christian formation (Chapter 9)
14. Balancing affirmation of contemporary society with the call-
    ing to be countercultural for the gospel (Chapter 7).

4 Examples of this variance are given in Chapter 10.

4

PART I

Roots and Shoots

I

Our Story and God's Story

I have been all things unholy. If God can work through me, God can work through anyone.

St Francis of Assisi

Mark's story

In the mid-nineties I took what I thought would be time out from my career as a theatrical lighting designer to train as a youth minister. This change of direction meant that I spent many an hour in Christian bookshops looking to fill my shelves with theology and ministry books. In these bookshops there always seemed to be a high-profile section full of what they called Celtic Christianity. I don't think I ever saw more images of rainbows over beaches and ruined castles in a misty landscape! As well as the core subjects of my training course, we had occasional visiting speakers, one of whom came to talk to us about this 'rediscovery' of Celtic spirituality. As I sat and listened I got more and more annoyed with what I saw as a load of romantic nonsense. I could not see how this was at all relevant to me or the kids from South London I had been working with. It just looked like the latest middle-class Christian fad. Yes, the poetry was lovely and the imagery at times beautiful, but it felt so disconnected from what life must have been like at that time and from what life was like now. I thought the only way for me to put to bed my growing frustration was to find out the real story. So my wife and I took a flight to Dublin, booked a little B&B and spent a week travelling around the Republic of Ireland, following lines of High Crosses, visiting sites and learning what we could about the culture and people of these early monastic communities.

What we encountered as we travelled was something far wilder, more extreme and harder than the modern interpretation of Celtic Christianity. In a tiny visitor centre in County Cavan we learned about St Killian, who took the gospel to Bavaria and was murdered for his trouble when he challenged a duke in Würzburg about his marriage. In Glendalough we learned about St Kevin, who established a community in the hard countryside of County Wicklow and is reported to have stood naked up to his chest for days in the freezing waters of the lake praying. We learned about St Brendan, who is said to have set sail in a fishing boat on a journey across the Atlantic Ocean that would take seven years. These, and many other stories of wild and somewhat crazy men and women (for we also discovered that many of the communities included men and women, even families), seemed to have no connection with the soft, romantic version of Celtic Christianity peddled by some of today's writers. Perhaps these people did have something to say to our present-day culture about commitment to God, about community and about mission after all.

One evening I was running a youth club in my training church, when a man riding a Vespa scooter pulled up in front of the adjacent house. I have always had a passion for Italian scooters, so I went to speak with him. He invited me to meet him and some friends of his at a local pub on the following Sunday. When I arrived I was the only one there, but after a while a tall, well-built skinhead walked through the door. He was dressed head to toe in black, apart from his red braces, and on the arm of his jacket were a large number of badges which gave away his political allegiances, including to the then leading far right group, the National Front. I tried to look the other way, but he spotted me and began to walk over. As he approached me he reached out his hand and said, 'Hi Mark, glad you could make it.' This was the man I'd met, now divested of his waterproofs and crash helmet. As others joined us I realized that his political views were not in a minority in the group! I had a decision to make; I could make my excuses and leave, or stay and be very uncomfortable. I decided to stay and for the next two years I spent time with the group, taking part in their joys – their weddings and the birth of their children

– and their sorrows. For these people church simply wasn't something they thought about and no matter what changes were made to what church looked like, they were not going to go.

After completing my training I went to minister in a large church in South London which was very successful and in many ways self-sufficient. We had a thriving group of young people, very creative youth worship events and great relationships with other youth groups. But there was little engagement with young people outside the church: to be honest we didn't need that! In my second year in post I received a phone call from the vicar of the neighbouring parish, a smaller, more traditional church that had been the original village church. A young boy from the large school in the parish had committed suicide on the anniversary of his father's own suicide. Young people were leaving notes in the church and the vicar wanted to ask me what I thought he should do. I suggested buying a big block of Post-it-Notes and a box of pens and leaving the church open. He did this and within a few days the altar was covered with messages from the young people, some words of anger, some of grief and some prayers. These young people had had no obvious context in which to express their feelings and their grief, but they needed to nevertheless.

These two stories are examples of how my thinking about mission and the Church has been shaped over the years. I began to look to those who sought to live out their faith in the midst of the communities of others. Those early British 'peregrinate', Celtic holy wanderers, came to inspire me more and more. In 2005 my wife and I moved to Telford to found safespace, a new Christian community. The aim was to explore what a Christian community might look like in a post-Church culture and to engage in mission among those for whom church had no relevance. Our vision was to identify ourselves as wanderers, and grow a community that did not want to increase by attracting others, but wanted always to ask how we live our lives as guests in the wider community and culture. It would be a community that helped all its members to live this way, by supporting, challenging and serving each other. New monasticism for safespace has never been a goal or an ending; for us it has been an ongoing attempt to engage with the immensity of a God who is 'out there', yet who is present within our culture. We desired to walk with God as individuals but more importantly as a community.

Ian's story

In my book *God Unknown*, I talked about a growing awareness of God's presence through art, feelings in the guts and through experience, or what I called the 'trans-rational' (knowing God through experience rather than knowing God just through rational facts about God). This was the beginning of a ten-year pilgrimage in experiencing and seeking after God the Trinity, not as some form of overly and stuffy academic or elitist head-knowledge, but a hunger to experience and understand the implications of the heart of the Christian faith. However, as I reflect now on how I ended up a new monastic Christian, I remember there were other important elements that began with a hunger for deep spiritual community and communion with God. Mysticism as a deep connection with God became a yearning.

At the age of 17, my only experience of Christianity was religious knowledge at comprehensive school, a local charismatic Baptist church and *Songs of Praise* on the TV. It was less than exhilarating. However, at the end of my first year of sixth-form college, I was invited by some friends to join them on a trip to the Taizé Community on the border between France and Switzerland. Not knowing what to expect, I found the whole experience full of awe, beauty, spirituality and deep humanity. I stayed for several months and the pattern of my day became a rhythm of work, prayer and chanted worship. The Brothers were very encouraging, and I found myself deeply enthralled by everything to do with the religious life. My cynicism about Christianity and negative stereotype had been challenged and replaced by a greater respect.

Twenty years later I became involved with the Moot Community, which was a fresh expression of church in Westminster. In a conversation with Steven Croft, then Archbishops' Missioner and Fresh Expressions Team Leader, he suggested in a moment of great wisdom, 'Have you thought about Moot developing a rhythm of life as a way to define and inspire a particular understanding of Christian discipleship?' That went right into the guts with a number of us, as it felt deeply of God and actually quite obvious. After a year of exploration, discernment and learning in dialogue with a number of new monastic communities, Moot developed its aspirations (aspirational statements about how we can seek to be Christians living an integrated and healthy life in, but not of, contemporary London society) to name its own sense of calling and vocation. What had begun as an alternative worship community had grown into an emerging church, and was now growing into a particular expression of a new monastic community. In that time we formed relationships with Anglican Franciscans and Benedictines seeking to work out if we were called to be more like monks or mendicant friars. These were beautiful and affirming conversations which helped the Moot Community to realize that we were part of the ongoing tradition of the religious life, but also something new in the sense that we were being called to be both monks and friars, and that many new monastics shared this dual vocation with a different form of spiritual rhythm or rule. The aspirations, the first level of our rhythm of life, sought to engage with the question, 'How should we live in, but not of, the culture of London?' A couple of years later the spiritual practices followed, defining our pattern of Christian discipleship, and the postures defining what it means for us to live a life of worship of God.

This journey felt totally natural and exciting. It really did feel as if we were following a path that God was revealing regarding our next steps. Now established for 11 years, Moot is meeting with a number of other new monastic communities charged with a new discernment, to set up a new Anglican New Monastic Acknowledged Religious Community (a designation given to Church of England religious communities who have a rule or rhythm of life but do not make the core vows of poverty, obedience and chastity), with a vision to grow a community of brothers and sisters not just in central London, but wherever God leads.

So new monasticism has become a key motif in my sense of vocation as a Christian and as an ordained priest seeking to serve a new monastic religious community of ordinary people called to be and do extraordinary things.

2

Old but New

While other Christian traditions have the monastic life, not all have a monastic spirit that is so readily accessible ... Thus, this monastic spirit becomes a gift that Anglicanism can offer back to the Church Catholic.[1]

In the last 20 years, new monastic communities have been bubbling up within the UK and beyond. In the UK these communities and their inherent missional orientation were recognized as a category of Fresh Expressions of Church as documented in the 'Mission-Shaped Church' Report.

A number of bishops in the Church of England have blessed and encouraged the birth and development of new monastic communities and the making of seasonal vows and aspirations. There is now much interest and support for nurturing and supporting new monastic small missional communities in this new mixed economy of the local church. Some may revitalize parish life and some, like traditional communities, will operate outside but in co-operation with diocese and parishes.

For this to work well, it is important that new monastics understand this ancient and future task, drawing on the wisdom of the tradition of monasticism and the religious life, and what this means in practice.

The Anglican inheritance in England

Some new monastic communities in England have a connection with the Anglican Church. Within the DNA of the Church of

---

1 Fr Jonathan, 2011, *The Anglican Way: The Monasticism of All Believers*, http://conciliaranglican.com/2011/07/13/the-anglican-way-the-Monasticism-of-all-believers/.

England is an important monastic inheritance. Among the chaos and violence of the Reformation, one of the greatest tragedies was the closure of the monastic and mendicant friar houses (which among others things were the welfare state of their time) causing starvation and death of the poor. However, the reforming vision for parish churches at the time of the dissolution of the monasteries saw the local church as the new accessible local monastery, as the locus for monastic prayer and worship. So the Church Commissioners of King Henry VIII stripped the monasteries of their resources, and expected parish churches to encourage a local rhythm of daily prayer, Holy Communion, loving service to the poor and participation in the local community. At the same time, cathedrals retained their monastic focused community and Daily Office so ensuring that the spirit of monasticism lived on.

A key element to the formation of the Anglican Church was the creation of the Book of Common Prayer under the auspices of Archbishop Thomas Cranmer. He was not a monk, but nevertheless the Book of Common Prayer became the standard for liturgy throughout the Church, and the monastic office was right at its heart. Cranmer took the seven times of day that monks and nuns prayed and reduced it down to two: Morning and Evening Prayer. In so doing, he made the monastic approach to prayer and spiritual discipline something that was both accessible to ordinary people and expected of the clergy. The Daily Office would no longer be for the privilege of closeted monks and nuns, it would now be a central aspect of the Christian life for everyone.[2]

However, the monastics had not been expunged forever. In the carnage and terrible working conditions of the Industrial Revolution of the nineteenth century, and in a time of weakening of the Church, the Oxford Movement led to a revival not only of mission, but of the re-creation of communities of the religious life. If you read accounts of the time, it is fascinating to see how the Church did not know what to do about the many people who discerned a vocation to become monks, nuns and friars, but who actually had a very hard time being accepted. There are many accounts of

---

2 Jonathan, *Anglican Way.*

the struggle of these new monastics recovering nineteenth-century re-creations of the way of St Benedict, St Clare and St Francis. They were clearly oppressed at the time, but the floodgates of this monastic missionary zeal could not be held back, and a number of new friar, nun and monk communities were reconstituted within the Church of England, which again pumped new vitality and purpose back into the Church in a time of major social change.

It is this monastic and mission-minded spirit that we think lies at the heart of new monasticism – a hunger for depth, love, community and service to God in the world. To explore this more fully we need to look further into the origins of monasticism, and explore the purpose and vision of some of the monastic and friar movements. To do this we will explore the historical contribution each has made to the ongoing tradition of monasticism, and listen to contemporary voices – to Abbot Stuart for the Anglican Benedictines and Brother Samuel for the Anglican Franciscans.

The origins of Christian monasticism

The words 'monk' and 'monasticism' find their root in the Greek word *monos*, meaning *alone*. The object of the 'solitary' was to confront the full mystery of the invisible God in silence.[3] Christian monasticism first emerged in the late third and early fourth centuries in hermitic form, where Christian women and men went into silence and contemplation in the deserts of Egypt and Syria. They were inspired to do so, following the Gospel stories about Jesus Christ seeking God in the desert, as well as Jesus' demand for self-denial in his appeal to the rich young man to sell his possessions and give the proceeds to the poor.[4]

An early example of this ascetic life is Anthony of Egypt (c. 251–356), who went with his sister into the Egyptian desert.[5]

---

3 E. Glenn Hinson, 1995, *The Church Triumphant: A History of Christianity up to 1300*, Macon: Mercer University Press, p. 123.

4 Hinson, *Church Triumphant*, p. 122.

5 Most of what is known about St Anthony comes from the *Life of Anthony*, written in Greek around 360 by Athanasius of Alexandria.

They attracted a number of followers and formed monastic communities, and became known as the desert mothers and fathers. Some left for the desert to escape religious persecution in the Roman Empire, some to avoid discriminatory tax burdens or even compulsory civic service.[6] In time the growing numbers led to the establishment of a more cenobitic or 'communitarian' form of monasticism which stresses community life.[7]

These hermitic and cenobitic forms of monasticism were solely of lay people. In fact, they took strong exception to anyone who sought ordained priesthood, as an early reaction against increasing clericalization in the Church. In quite a short time these desert monastic communities grew, starting monastic movements in North Africa, Eastern Europe, later in Western Europe, and eventually among the Celtic peoples of Northern Europe. This early monastic movement drew heavily on the teachings and spiritual disciplines of the desert mothers and fathers including Anthony of Egypt.

Central to this form of monasticism was the call to prayer. They recited the Lord's Prayer as 'the method and form of prayer proposed by God'. They chanted the psalms, repeating the prayer of Psalm 70.1, 'O God, make speed to save me; O Lord, make haste to help me', as central to a daily cycle. They developed the Jesus Prayer ('Lord Jesus Christ, Son of God, have mercy on me a sinner'), reciting it as an anchor for meditation. In the midst of prayer, they were committed to the common life of shared work, food preparation, hospitality, and religious instruction.[8]

From these desert beginnings, monasticism spread throughout the Roman Empire, eventually leading to the development of a variant strain of monasticism developing in France and the British Isles. It is a particularly Celtic expression of monasticism that supported Patrick and the evangelization of Ireland. The Christian evangelization of Britain in the Romano-Celtic and Anglo-Saxon

6 John Finney, 1998, *Recovering the Past: Celtic and Roman Mission*, London: Darton, Longman and Todd, pp. 50–2.

7 Finney, *Recovering*, p. 51.

8 Hinson, *Church Triumphant*, pp. 124–5.

eras occurred through the missional endeavours of monks, nuns and friars, rather than bishops, priests and parishes.

From Ireland, monastic Christian evangelism spread north to the Scots, and Scotland was evangelized (a key role being played by the monastery on the Isle of Iona), and through the creation of the Community of Lindisfarne, northern and central England were evangelized. At the same time, southern England was evangelized by missionary monastics sent from Rome. What we know as Celtic monasticism had much in common with European monasticism, but did differ in approach, influenced by Byzantine monasticism from the East and famously its use of the calendar, particularly the way in which the date of Easter was calculated.

These Celtic monk-wanderers (called the peregrinate) were responsible for the re-evangelization of many parts of Western Europe after the fall of the Roman Empire.[9]

> The peregrinate enabled the Celtic monastic movement to move fast and far [in the sixth to eighth centuries]. They often travelled in groups. Where they stopped they evangelised and maintained as far as possible their monastic life of prayer and contemplation. If their mission to the area bore fruit they would settle and a new monastery would be born. The process can be most easily seen in the Columbanian communities of Northern Gaul ... Some like Luxeuil were large communities, but there must have been many others where only a few brothers or sisters lived a common life in humble dwellings.[10]

By taking this approach, Celtic monastics instigated what we would now consider both a contextual and incarnational 'church planting' model. After the Synod of Whitby in the seventh century (at which the Celtic church submitted to the ecclesial authority and practice of Rome), this model of mission and ministry changed.

---

9 Finney, *Recovering the Past*, pp. 56–8.
10 Finney, *Recovering the Past*, p. 57.

The competition of traditions [Roman and Celtic] is quite visible in English monastic history. The earliest monks came from Ireland to Iona, bringing with them the powerful mission- ary impulse and more rigorous form of Christianity with its emphasis upon self-examination and penance. From Iona the Celtic tradition spread to Lindisfarne and took hold in North- umbria. Not long afterwards, however, Gregory the Great sent Augustine and a group of [Roman] monks from the Monastery of St Andrew ... Introduction of the Benedictine Rule came by way of Wilfrid, who had been brought up at Lindisfarne but had become familiar with the Rule of Benedict in several trips to Gaul on his way to Rome.[11]

Celtic monasticism and the peregrinate did not die out immedi- ately but struggled on for a while. It seems that Celtic monasticism was in part killed off by Viking raiders – Iona, Lindisfarne and other coastal monasteries were all ransacked. It was in the end subsumed, sometimes forcibly, by the increasingly powerful Roman expression of monasticism. Only at the Synod of Whitby was Celtic monasticism formally subordinated to Western, Euro- pean monasticism in England, Scotland and Wales.

Benedictine monasticism

Abbot Stuart Burns is the Abbot of Mucknell Abbey, a Benedictine community founded in the aftermath of the Oxford Movement, wonderfully called The Society of the Salutation of Mary the Virgin. For Abbot Stuart, monasticism is about a calling to live the religious life: a rhythm of prayer, contemplation, work and rest defined by the rule of St Benedict, an abbot in the sixth century. Benedict would have remained obscure, if it were not for the writings of Gregory the Great, himself a monastic who became a bishop of Rome.[12] Benedict was a reformer. He was passionate about the importance of lay communities empowered

---

11 Hinson, *Church Triumphant*, p. 321.
12 Finney, *Recovering the Past*, pp. 64–6.

OLD BUT NEW

with monastic principles, and about re-establishing a credible form and practice of the Christian faith. He founded a monastery in Monte Cassino in Italy, which became one of the leading monastic communities in Western Europe of its time.

The gift of Benedictine monasteries was that they were catalysts for evangelism, discipleship and mission in Western Europe. Much of what we would see as crucial in the modern world – such as education, health care, welfare, libraries, patronage of the arts, and community cohesion – find their beginnings in the monastics. Benedictine places of hospitality became hospitals, and community refectories became soup kitchens. The Benedictine tradition raised many pioneers and visionaries that, from the sixth century, helped the Church to face social and cultural change, amid a time of sustained war and religious conquest in Europe which had catastrophic social consequences of persecution, disease, starvation, dispossession from the land, and death. Most of all, they were essential for the support and survival of the very poorest in society. This approach to discipleship was expressed through a written rule of life developed by Benedict. As Louis Bouyer (a French Lutheran minister who converted to Catholicism in 1939 and was part of the International Theological Commission in 1969) has said, this approach is both mystical and radical:

As the rule of St Benedict so forcefully emphasizes, it is finally, the search for God – seeking to meet God and to meet God immediately – taking hold of everything in us and doing away with everything else for us: this search and this alone constitutes the meaning of the monastic life and justifies its renouncements. Certainly, every Christian must seek God. But the monk is possessed by the desire to find God and with so great an urgency that they abandon everything else for its sake ... Let us make it clear once again that this abandonment of all things is only provisional: in seeking God, we cannot help also seeking [God's] Kingdom, God's universal Kingdom.[13]

13 Louis Bouyer, 1961, *Introduction to Spirituality*, Collegeville, MN: Liturgical Press, p. 194.

Benedict created a revised pattern of life for a monastic community around worship, prayer, work and rest, that drew on the best of a number of pre-existing monastic movements. This Benedictine revision became popular because it was straightforward and clear. As with all rules, it was constructed to be a guide to help people answer the question *How should we live?* The rule itself is expressed through 73 chapters – but the main points are summarized here:

1. *Defining types of monastics:* Benedict offers four different types of monks – *Cenobites*, those in set monasteries under a spiritual rule with the oversight of an abbot; *Hermits*, those after long training living in solitude; *Sarbeites*, those living in twos or threes with no rule or oversight; and *Gyrovagues*, wandering monks who move from monastery to monastery.[14]
2. *Setting abbots within a community structure:* Abbots need to treat their communities well, where everyone is equal without hierarchy and where everyone is consulted equally when implementing new ideas and changes. Obedience to an abbot is expected. *Deans* (from Latin *decanus*, 'relating to ten') are also assigned oversight of ten monks.
3. *Offering definitions of work:* Benedict defines 73 areas of work needed to sustain a monastic community. These are essentially the duties of every Christian and are mainly scriptural, whether in letter or in spirit. Sharing work in the kitchen is a given. The hours of labour vary with the season but are never fewer than five hours a day.
4. *Balancing talking and silence:* Talking in the monastic community is encouraged but to be moderated, and not banned.
5. *Offering a pattern of prayer and worship:* The Divine Office, a set of prayers and biblical readings (including the psalms) are prescribed through the year, with eight times of common prayer and worship each day. The Book of the Hours is an expression of this. Worship is seen as the reverence owed to

---

14 In his writings, Benedict clearly thinks that only cenobite and sarbeite monks are truly authentic and is scornful of the rest.

the omnipresent God. Prayer must be made with heartfelt passion and is not to be too wordy.

6. *Focusing on humility as the outcome of spiritual growth:* Humility is seen as a key quality to be developed, with 12 stages in becoming more humble.

7. *Prescribing living arrangements:* Each monk is to have a separate bed and room or cell, and is to sleep in his habit, so as to be ready to rise without delay for services. A permanent light is prescribed to burn in the dormitory throughout the night.

8. *Defining the ground rules of community living:* Governance is strict, and the rule expresses a process of growth, which if not adhered to, would result in having to leave the monastery. Monks are allowed to leave three times before they are barred permanently.

9. *Offering an alternative to materialism:* Private possessions are banned, but the abbot is duty bound to provide all necessities. Receiving letters is banned without the abbot's permission.

10. *Dealing with illness:* When a monastic is sick, there are prescribed dispensations, particularly around food.

11. *Offering hospitality:* Guests are to be met with due courtesy by the abbot, abbess or his or her deputy; during their stay they are to be under the special protection of an appointed monk or nun; they are not to associate with the rest of the community except by special permission.

12. *Offering ethical fundraising:* For all things made or crafted at the community, they need to be sold at or below the market price, and never above the market price.

13. *Offering a sustainable monastic life:* The rule sustains a rhythm of life of work, worship, prayer and rest.

14. *Offering a framework for beginners:* An epilogue at the end of the rule declares that the rule is not offered as an ideal of perfection, but merely as a means towards godliness, intended chiefly for novices in the spiritual life.

For Abbot Stuart, the Benedictine rule has much to offer new monastics in the twenty-first century, as it has resourced Christians and spiritual seekers in earlier times. Such a rule enables people to explore their own spiritual journey, with the advantage that it could act as a guide for Christian spiritual communities to work out how they exist and affirm what is good in contemporary culture but also how they can be countercultural to the materialism, greed and inhumanity that is also present in society. In so doing, new monastics draw on the strengths of the Benedictine tradition to be distinctively Christian. A good example is the Benedictine expectation that their monks will be good listeners and loving in all their interaction with people. This practice can only be maintained by a healthy spiritual life of prayer and contemplation where each individual seeks to live out a virtuous life instead of greed, fear, anger and selfishness.

Monasticism based on the Benedictine rule offers a positive expression of faith. It seeks to promote the Christian God as a loving deity, and where all love proceeds from God. This reflects the apostle Paul's second letter to the Corinthians, chapter 5, where the author articulates an understanding of God reconciling all things back into restored relationship through Christ. This cosmic vision shows the restorative purposes of God through love. This God calls all Christians to participate in this love mission to the world.

For a Benedictine, Christ's new commandment to love God, love one another and love others as yourself is central to the Christian identity. Abbot Stuart agrees with his Roman Catholic Benedictine counterpart, Christopher Jamison (former Abbot of Worth Abbey, who featured in the BBC Two documentary, *The Monastery* and author of *Finding Sanctuary: Monastic steps for Everyday Life* and *Finding Happiness: Monastic Steps for a Fulfilling Life*[15]), who summarizes this calling as being 'True to God, True to yourself, and True to Others.'[16]

Abbot Stuart is convinced that Benedict's rule was grounded in an expectation that monks experience the love of God as an

15 Christopher Jamison, 2007, *Finding Sanctuary: Monastic Steps for Everyday Life*, Phoenix: Orion Publishing; 2008, *Finding Happiness: Monastic Steps for a Fulfilling Life*, Phoenix: Orion Publishing.
16 Jamison, *Finding Sanctuary*.

affirming deity motivated by love. Once people know they are loved by God, they are more likely to face their brokenness, inspired by the unconditional love of Father, Son and Spirit.

Abbot Stuart shares this vision with many new monastics: that the Christian story and faith is about hope, grace, and seeking a God of love (which he finds increasingly distorted by the more angry and fundamentalist expressions of faith and church). In a complete challenge to this, the Benedictine rule can be interpreted as starting with a call to 'love God with all your heart, mind and soul', and then to love your neighbour or others through practices inspired with the values of the Beatitudes (Matthew 5.3–12; Luke 6.20–23). In this tradition Abbot Stuart focuses on inclusion, in seeking to imitate Christ, who in the Gospels talked, ate and drank with many people who were excluded from religious society. He sees the Benedictine approach as a particular way to live as an expression of the early church – maintaining a common purse, sharing resources, and seeking to be a visible community embodying the values of the invisible kingdom of God.

The Mucknell Abbey community is an interesting example of the challenge facing the Church in the cultural shift from religion to spirituality. The Benedictine community he oversees has moved out of its old Jacobean buildings near Oxford to a new site near Worcester Abbey. Abbot Stuart led the community in the building of a totally new Abbey focused on social and ecological justice, utilizing sustainable low carbon forms of energy including wind, solar and thermal power. Drawing on the depths of the Benedictine monastic tradition, Abbot Stuart and his monastic community are regenerating or evolving their mission to serve people who are spiritually searching, and who may want to live with the community for a while. This form of radical hospitality, allowing people to belong to the community, participating in its life, and then being able to explore the Christian faith (what some have called *belonging before believing*) is faithful to the ongoing monastic tradition.

The Benedictine tradition reminds us of the importance of a focus on life. Such an approach is about seeking and knowing God in the context of pain and suffering, and the struggle of the reality of life, and a dogged commitment to seek God in it, even when God seems absent.

New monasticism, inspired by the Benedictine tradition with its communitarian focus on love and life, on living out life together as an ecclesial community with and to the world, challenges the dualism of many contemporary expressions of the Christian faith. The world is not a broken God-less place, and the human body is not a nasty, sinful thing our pure souls need to escape from. The cosmos is God-breathed and sustained and is beautiful, and we in our enfleshedness have been created in the image of God as an original blessing that, yes, acknowledges brokenness, but where we are firmly loved by God.

The coming of the mendicant friars

The thirteenth century saw the flowering of the four great mendicant friar orders ('mendicant' from the Latin *mendicans* meaning 'begging', a member of a religious order combining monastic life and outside religious activity and originally owning neither personal nor community property), responding to the mission and ministry needs of medieval Europe. St Francis with the support of St Clare of Assisi founded the Order of Friars Minor in 1209, known as the 'Grey Friars', and St Dominic founded an order of teaching and preaching friars in 1216,[17] the Order of Preachers, also known as the 'Black Friars'. The Carmelites formed friars blessed by the Bishop of Rome in 1245 who spread contemplative forms of prayer called the 'White Friars', and the Augustinians ('Austin Friars') were also constituted in 1245.

All were wanderers, particularly the Franciscan friars:

Saint Francis established The Order of Friars Minor ... With their love of poverty and spontaneity, the Franciscan movement has brought colour and compassion into many a market place.

---

17 Ray Simpson, 2009, *High Street Monasteries: Fresh Expressions of Committed Christianity*, Stowmarket: Kevin Mayhew, p. 52.

Unlike monastics, these are travelling mendicants with a vow of Poverty.[18]

The word *friar* derives from the French word *frère* and Latin *frater*, both meaning 'brother'. Such language borrows the practice of the early church to see all Christians as sisters and brothers in the new extended family where God is the heavenly Father, Abba. Friars were commissioned for public service drawing on a rhythm of life, while monks were more about withdrawal, prayer and contemplation.[19]

Like the Benedictine monks before them, St Francis and the other friar-pioneers began their orders in response to a Church that was increasingly over-clericalized with a growing gap between the Church and contemporary culture. Many ordinary people gravitated to medieval sects rather than the Church, so the friars in their open and evangelistic approach sought to reform the Church and enable people to relate and belong to it. The friars can be seen as a missional response to major social change. At the time, all across Europe, many people moved from arable farming in the country to learning trades in cities and towns, which became centres for the new guilds that were increasingly estranged from the Church. So the friars promoted a new form of Christian mission and evangelism with the birth of radical new communities of faith, remaining obedient to and collaborative with the wider Church.

Franciscan friar mendicant communities

To help understand the particularly Franciscan contribution to the story of religious orders, we met with Brother Samuel, who was the Minister Provincial for the European Province of the Anglican Franciscans. Brother Samuel views Francis as a contemplative, mystic and activist. For him the uniqueness of Franciscanism is

---

18 Simpson, *High Street Monasteries*, p. 52.
19 Hinson, 1995, *Church Triumphant*, pp. 450–2.

emphasized in St Francis' passion for the incarnation, the humanity of Christ and the beautiful mystery of God sharing human life.

> Franciscanism is a very Christ-centred spirituality. The emphasis then is on the goodness of life, and the spiritual awareness of the goodness, love and generosity of God, which is present through all creation. The Franciscan theologians that came after Francis develop this theme further, particularly the writing of Duns Scotus and Bonaventure. For them, not only was the goodness of God present to us through creation, but that the world was pregnant with God, in everything you see, taste and touch. Everything that is beautiful is close to God.[20]

For Franciscans, Jesus being fully human and fully God was the fulfilment of creation. In some Christian theology, Jesus as redeemer is seen as the rescue effort, but for Franciscans the incarnation is the focus of God's purposes and design from the beginning. For Franciscans the details of the life of Christ as recorded in the Gospels were the main inspiration for life – attempting to follow the teachings of Jesus, and to experience the world with openness as Christ did. Franciscans seek to follow the *Logos* ('the Word became flesh' as recorded in the Gospel of John) who becomes human in Christ. So from the start, Christ is seen to be loving and humble. God did not come as a king, but as a servant, and calls Christians to follow in this calling to loving service and humility.

Francis, enjoying the racy, privileged life, as a playboy son of a wealthy mercantile family, increasingly began to recognize an emerging sense of calling to the religious life. In contrast to many of his contemporaries, he did not join a traditional monastic community. Through a deeply ongoing contemplative and mystical experience of Christ present through the world and in his life, Francis began as a hermit. From there, Francis followed his inclinations on his own spiritual path, to start something new:

> Instead of accepting one of the well-established forms of Christian life available in the early 1200s, he chose the more

---

20 As recorded in an interview between the authors and Brother Samuel SSF.

difficult way, creating a new 'form of life, as he called it ...
[driven by the] desire to create something new [which] was his
deep conviction that it was 'the Lord Jesus Christ' himself who
was guiding him. Followers soon arrived: 'The Lord gave me
brothers,' he said. They formed a fraternity, following a form
of life based on the Gospel. In part contemplatives, in part popular preachers, they lived by the work of their hands, frequently
with the sick, and begged when they needed to.[21]

For Francis, being a spiritual community meant obedience to
Christ and participation in the world. Initially, the rhythm of life
for this community meant following the inspiration of Christ's
life in the Gospels. It was a radical form of spiritual community,
concerned with engagement with the world, entering its brokenness rather than creating monastic withdrawal. This approach to
life is centred on contemplation and action.

Reading the stories of Francis, we meet a man who was deeply
moved by encountering Christ through events, people and nature.
As a mystic and contemplative, Francis shared this sensibility with
Benedictines; God was the source of all love.

Under pressure from the early Franciscan communities, Francis
developed a four-point rule to help give a focus to Franciscan
spirituality. The purpose of the rule was to promote a life that
praises God in and through all things, joining in with the praise
of all creation to know and serve God even in the most humble,
lowly and marginal situations, serving both people and creatures.
Francis outlined four elements of the vocation of a friar:

1. Living as relational Brothers – by knowing Brother Jesus we
   seek to become brothers with all people – living in fraternity
   with others and creation.
2. Living as Lesser Brothers – knowing the importance of humility. Choosing powerlessness and living this way, following
   Jesus who had a serving and loving vocation.

---

21 William J. Short, 1999, *Poverty and Joy*, Maryknoll, NY: Orbis Books, p. 21.

3. Living as peacemaking Brothers – being an instrument of peace. Bringing reconciliation, and living as an agent of political peace and inner peace.
4. Living as mission-centred Brothers – proclaiming the gospel by living it. Francis is famous for the saying attributed to him, 'Preach the gospel at all times, and when necessary, use words.'

Like the Benedictines before him, Francis saw the need to be a radical community, but understood the necessity of being part of, and authorized by, the wider Church.

After the first group of brothers numbered twelve, they asked for and received a verbal approval of their way of life from Pope Innocent III, who was doing the same for a number of new religious renewal movements at the time.[22]

Soon after this approval, the new Franciscan community was recognized as the religious Order of Lesser Brothers or 'Friars Minor' whose rule soon included learned members and priests.

One of the greatest achievements of Franciscanism has been its attentiveness to the importance of social, economic and ecological justice. In the stories of Francis, he is said to have travelled to the Holy Land at the time of the Crusades and, being appalled at the slaughter and violence, requested a private audience and dialogue with the Islamic Sultan. This story wonderfully illustrates the gospel values of loving your enemies, seeking reconciliation and a common humanity, even with those outside the Christian faith.

A commitment such as Francis' is of importance as we increasingly live in pluralistic and multicultural societies. That is a calling to be religiously exclusivist (having a clear belief in the Christian, Trinitarian God as the one God) while being politically pluralist (seeing the importance of people's freedom to practise whatever belief or religion they choose to).

Brother Samuel confirmed his understanding of the distinction between the vocation of Benedictine monastics and Franciscan mendicants. However, he also recognized that they had a family

---

22 Short, 1999, *Poverty and Joy*, p. 28.

likeness, and that there were close bonds of affection between them.

For both the Franciscan mendicants and Benedictine monastics, contemplative spirituality is fundamentally important to an understanding of living the Christian faith. Both Benedict and Francis did not intend to found religious orders, being more interested in living a life reflective of the gospel. During their lifetimes, this was a new approach and one which inspired mission and renewal of the wider Church engaging with contemporary culture.

When asked what elements of Franciscanism might be unhelpful for being Christian in the twenty-first century, Brother Samuel responded by urging us to avoid superficial understandings of St Francis by a romanticism about Francis being best friends with animals and the earth: 'too much emphasis on romantic mysticism rather than the guts of his way of life. You can have the outward forms of the religious life, without having the inner spirituality of it, which then becomes superficial.' Brother Samuel said this was a great danger. There needed to be a deep spirituality.

When asked what he thought of new monasticism, Brother Samuel became passionate about its importance for Christian faith in the twenty-first century:

I believe it to be very authentic. In a time when most religious orders in the Western Church are facing decline and extinction, new monasticism reflects a whole new eruption of different forms of the religious life. This is what we see in the history of the Church, that the religious life keeps reinventing itself, or put another way, the Holy Spirit is moving people to live the gospel in this particularly focused way, which has common themes of a life of community or association which is more than what you get in some forms of church ... the importance of relational obligation, the centrality of a daily rhythm of prayer and worship as a spiritual discipline. As I understand it, many new monastics follow a long history of religious orders that are committed to the sharing of resources, property, gifts and the common purpose of the community.[23]

---

23 Telephone interview.

The beginnings of a new monasticism

From the time of the Franciscans onwards, expressions of the Christian religious life have bubbled up as renewal movements around the world in all traditions of church. It could be argued that the Protestant Evangelical tradition itself was created out of the carnage of the Reformation drawing on an interpretation of Benedictine spirituality. After all, Luther was a monk. However, the language of a new monasticism finds a number of roots that have grown into a worldwide network and, in some ways, a disconnected movement.

The Oxford Movement in the nineteenth century began as a reaction to the weakening of the Church of England as the established church. The crisis created a dynamic response birthing new mission initiatives around the UK and beyond, giving rise to the Anglo-Catholic Anglican tradition now widely expressed around the world. What is often not known, is the incredible resurgence of new forms of monasticism and religious life that were re-established in the Church of England 500 years after the abolition of the monasteries under Henry VIII. New Anglican religious communities were founded in the USA, Canada, Australia, New Zealand, Africa and the South Pacific. At first this was a struggle. If we learn anything from the Oxford Movement, it is from the stories of just how hard it was and is to be listened to and taken seriously regarding mission and a new monasticism. Many monastic pioneers in the nineteenth century could not get adequate permission to re-found religious communities for those who felt called to a renewal of the vocation to the religious life led by an obviously mission-minded Holy Spirit. Luckily for us the opposition from powerful church authorities could not hold back the floodgates of God's intentions. It was the lack of a generous ecclesiology and missiology among parish priests, archdeacons and bishops of the Church of England that made this so difficult. But many new religious communities were re-founded, and these have made a major contribution to Church and society around the world.

Following the great social upheavals of the First and Second

World Wars, all sorts of small communities of a new monastic orientation were birthed. Dietrich Bonhoeffer and his friends started a number of radical Lutheran new monastic communities in opposition to the Third Reich. These held a shared rhythm of life and intentional community (living together) which sought to take in those who were being persecuted by the regime. Nearly all members of these communities were shot or sent to concentration camps. After the Second World War the Iona Community began out of a desire for a more integrated Christian spirituality that included eco-spirituality and justice and set up a new intentional community on the island and has grown an international family. On Lindisfarne a similar community birthed the 'Aidan and Hilda' new monastic community network, which is now global.

More recently in the late twentieth and early twenty-first century dissatisfaction among Western Christians concerned with just living, a lack of a loving and missionary spirit and desire for greater relational community has given rise to the language of new monasticism. In the USA a number of leading new monastic communities were established in the late 1990s. These included the 'Simple Way Community' and the work and writings of Shane Claiborne in Philadelphia, and the 'Rubta' Community in Durham and the work and writings of Jonathan Wilson-Hartgrove. In 2004 new monastic communities gathered in the USA to affirm what they called the 'Twelve Marks of New Monasticism'[24] which led to the flourishing of a new movement, with many new communities being birthed in the USA, Canada and Europe as a result.

At the same time as new monasticism was taking off in the USA, the Fresh Expressions movement began in the UK. Following the decline of the Church in the 1990s the Fresh Expressions initiative was born as a mission-minded renewal movement that began in the UK in the Church of England, and quickly became a partnership between Anglicans, Methodists, United Reformed Church and more recently the Church of Scotland. In a key founding Church of England report, the 'Mission-Shaped Church' Report,[25] new monasticism was named as one of the important

---

24 As recorded at http://en.wikipedia.org/wiki/New_Monasticism.
25 See www.chpublishing.co.uk/uploads/documents/0715140132.pdf.

fresh expressions of church that needed to be nurtured and supported to enable effective mission and evangelism today. Many
new monastic communities have been born out of this initiative.
Fresh Expressions as a movement is now spread throughout the
worldwide Anglican Communion, and new monastic communities are now growing up within it.

Outside the Protestant Anglican tradition there are a number
of lay Roman Catholic movements that contain the DNA of a
new monasticism. In South America a number of lay Roman
Catholic ecclesial communities have been born in the context of
brutal social repression of the poor. These communities have a
particular focus on social justice, known as Liberation Theology.
The writings and works of leaders such as Gustavo Gutiérrez,
Leonardo Boff and Jon Sobrino have given rise to a number of
these more liberationist new monastic expressions of church. It
is true to say that these forms of church have been largely unsup-
ported and repressed by the Vatican until recently.

In Africa too, the Roman Catholic St Egidio community, which
is more of a new monastic lay order, has planted many lay new
monastic communities around the world. These are focused on
supporting the poor and reconciliation, particularly in the context of war and genocide. It will be interesting to see whether
the appointment of a new Jesuit pope (the Society of Jesus is a
religious order) will see an increased flourishing of new monasticism in the Roman Catholic Church.

Final reflections

In our discussions with Abbot Stuart and Brother Samuel there
has been broad agreement that there is a growing convergence
between contemporary monastics and mendicants. Regarding
their activity, many of those called to be monastics now have
times when they are being monks and other times when they
are being more friar-like, and there is now a lot of co-operation
between modern monastic and mendicant orders. For example,
the Franciscans at Hillfield Friary in Dorset have a man staying

with them who is learning about the religious life before moving to a Benedictine abbey to take up the vows of a monk.

The language of new monasticism may be growing because of this increased convergence of different orders of monastics and mendicants. Both traditions emphasize an understanding of the Christian life as *Life in the Spirit*. Both give room for people to explore their own spiritual journey, to discern where God appears to be calling them. This is the rich inheritance that traditional religious orders pass on to new monasticism; the place of love and the awareness of the Holy Spirit leading people on their own unique spiritual journey.

Ecological justice and stewardship is as important for traditional monastics and mendicants as it is for new monastics. Brother Samuel said:

> Particularly in our present age, I think we have a massive crisis with our relationship between modern society and creation or the environment. We are only just waking up to this need. We need a radical change of relationship with the world around us. Francis has a lot to teach us on this. In a culture where the whole economic system in which we live and have trusted, has failed and needs to be questioned, Francis says something radically different and with a vital perspective. He speaks and lives the economy of gift, not of the market. He offers a very powerful alternative, an economics and ecology centred on spiritual reconciliation.[26]

When asked what advice they would give to new monastics both Abbot Stuart and Brother Samuel affirmed that new monasticism was drawing on a wide number of the traditions of monks, nuns and friars, and that this was more than acceptable. Brother Samuel said:

> Do not worry too much about what you are doing, whether it is monk or friar. You will draw on both traditions, people always have. So draw and make connections with both because, in the

---

26 As recorded in interview between authors and Brother Samuel SSF.

end, if it is authentic, you will be called to do something radically new. There needs to be a deep sense of purpose behind whatever you do. Being a monastic or a friar is not an end in itself; it needs to be deeper than that. To be among the poor and witness to the poor will result on you drawing on the Franciscan inheritance. When you are focused more on prayer, praise and worship then you will draw on the Benedictine inheritance. What you must do is to keep facing the question, *What is God calling you to be? What are you about?* Keep seeking God for the vocation of your community. Things die and lose their way because they forget what they are about. Keeping any organization going is not an end in itself. Never get into the habit of doing things for the sake of it as there is no life-giving potential in this.[27]

---

27 Ibid.

3

Followers of the Holy Trinity

By the word of the Lord the heavens were made, their starry host by the breath of his mouth.

Psalm 33.6

Leonardo Boff, the Brazilian theologian, who had been a member of the Roman Catholic Franciscan order until his support of the liberation theologians meant that he was forced out of the Catholic Church, wrote:

> To say that God is communion means that the three Eternal ones, Father, Son and Holy Spirit, are turned toward one another. Each divine Person goes out of self and surrenders to the other two, giving life, love, wisdom, goodness and everything possessed. The Persons are distinct not in order to be separated but to come together and to be able to give themselves to one another. In the beginning is not the solitude of a One, of an eternal Being, alone and infinite. Rather, in the beginning is the communion of three Unique Ones. Community is the deepest and most foundational reality that exists.[1]

Community is an easy word to trot out, we all want to be in community. But there is a deep meaning to the word community and it is not found in a grouping of people I like who are like me. It is not contained in a criteria-bound club, a task and finish group or even sometimes in family. Where then is it found? In 1988 Boff wrote *Holy Trinity, Perfect Community* and the book was born from his struggle to understand how people could live together

1 Leonardo Boff, 2000, *Holy Trinity, Perfect Community*, Maryknoll, NY: Orbis Books, p. 3.

35

peacefully and creatively with God, on the earth. He opens with the question, 'Why get concerned today with the Blessed Trinity? It has been hard enough to believe in a single God. Believing in three Persons who are one God is much harder still!' and goes on to answer his own question, 'We never simply live, we always live together. Whatever favors shared life is good and worthwhile. Hence, it is worthwhile believing in this community style of God's existence, of God's trinitarian manner that is always communion and union of three.' For new monastic communities this desire to engage with a God who is by nature community is key. It underpins a sometimes anguished cry for 'real' community in the sea of a consumerist and individualistic culture. If community is not 'best practice', if community requires such hard work and at times pain, why do we yearn for it so? The Trinitarianism running through new monasticism grows from this sense that though community living is never easy it is part of who we are, made in the image of God.

For the safespace community this is extremely important:

For safespace being together around the table has always been where we have felt most ourselves, most at home. When we sit down we lose any pretence about status or pecking order, we face each other as equals, at the same level, young and old, male and female. All of us have contributed something to our meal together, however small. All of us have given of our time to cook, to set the table, to prepare a meditation, etc. As we come together from our daily struggles and commitments, we find rest and reality in community, indeed it is not unusual to hear an audible sigh travel around the room as each member takes their seat.[2]

Perhaps in this simple common act we can discover something of the deepest nature of God, that God is community. This is God as humble community, each part giving in to the whole, each part pointing always to the others. Not God as hierarchy, with Father as the CEO, Jesus as middle management and the Spirit

---

2 Content from interview.

on the factory floor (known as subordinationalism, the belief that God the Father is the greatest and most powerful among the members of the Trinity, followed by Christ and then the Holy Spirit); or one God with three different states of being (known as modalism, the belief that God is a single person who, throughout biblical history, has revealed himself in three modes, or forms); or even three independent gods (known as tritheism, the belief that the Godhead[3] is really three separate beings forming three separate gods); but God as the relationship between three different but interdependent persons. The Trinity as a radically mutual community, a community of the meal table, not the boardroom table! Theologians use the Greek term *perichoresis*, defined as co-participation, mutual indwelling and self-surrender, to describe this understanding of the nature of the Trinity.

Alister McGrath says that *perichoresis* 'allows the individuality of the persons to be maintained, while insisting that each person shares in the life of the other two. An image often used to express this idea is that of a "community of being," in which each person, while maintaining its distinctive identity, penetrates the others and is penetrated by them.'[4]

The Shield of the Trinity diagram helpfully places the word God at the centre, the point at which Father, Son and Spirit connect.

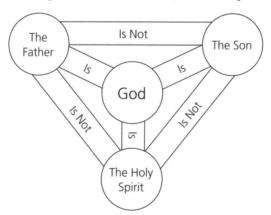

3 See http://carm.org/dictionary-godhead.

4 Alister McGrath, 2001, *Christian Theology: An Introduction*, 3rd edn, Oxford: Blackwell, p. 325.

It illustrates that Father, Son and Spirit are discrete and different but connected in relationship, indeed it is only in the intersecting of these relationships that we find the name God. Understanding the nature of God in this way is at the heart of how new monastic communities are seeking to be community and growing into a new romance with the God who is by nature community.

As God is one yet three expressing perfect love, justice and inclusion, so we the Church are beckoned so to do. John V. Taylor, former general secretary of the Church Missionary Society and Bishop of Winchester, an early critic of modern consumerism, wrote:

> Taking the Bible as a whole we can find no conception of man as an individual existing in and for himself, nor is its attention focused upon the individual's relation to God. The Christian can never truly say 'I am man', only 'I am in Man'; he exists not in his identity but in his involvement ... the blessings that are promised to those who maintain a right relationship with God are always communal, a share in the shalom, the peace of the People of God. For human destiny, according to the Bible, is the destiny of a 'people'.[5]

That the Christian community, the Church, is a community of participation is at the root of new monasticism. For safespace, this articulates their exploration of gifting within their community.

> As we 'perichoretically' surrender our God-given vocation, gifts and talents into the community they grow both in ourselves but also in the life of the whole community. This is changing how we see and do leadership within communities, where we put the emphasis on the flow of gifting and vocation rather than the authority of a title or position. Each of us surrenders our gifts to the community and so each of our gifts, rather than being lost becomes animated from use and spreads through the community. This may seem obvious but too often gifts are held

5 John V. Taylor, 2001, *The Primal Vision: Christian Presence amid African Religion*, London: SCM (SCM Classics), p. 77.

onto, both in terms of not offering them for the purpose of God and in elevating them in a spirit of pride. We have found that we need to use the gifts we have been blessed with, not for our own elevation or standing, not to gain for ourselves a role or sense of esteem but in order that others may use us and that they may themselves exercise the gift. Put simply when our prophets speak prophetically then we all in different ways hear God's call, when our artists create, we all find ourselves able to express ourselves better. As the whole community of God was involved in the work of the Creator (Psalm 33.6) so we all participate, if we are allowed to.[6]

Romans 8 takes this a step further. The community of God, the Trinity, is not only a model for growing healthy and life-giving community, it is also an invitation to participate in relationship and purpose. Paul Fiddes, described in 2002 as 'one of the leading contemporary Baptist theologians', writes:

> To participate in God means that there is the ever-present opportunity to be aligned with a movement of communication beyond ourselves which is pure love, and which is also a movement of the will. We can lean upon a movement which is a willing response of a son to a father, becoming co-actors and co-narrators with his 'Yes, amen' to the Father's purpose ... A triune doctrine of God encourages us to discover our roles as we participate in a God who is always in the movement of sending. The one who sends out the Son eternally from the womb of his being sends the Son into the world, and Christ after his resurrection from the dead says to his followers 'as the Father sent me, so I send you'. [7]

This understanding is at the core of new monasticism, the call to follow the way of Christ, to move into the neighbourhood in hope and love. For many communities this means relocating into the

---

6 Safespace, http://www.freshexpressions.org.uk/stories/safespace.

7 Paul Fiddes, 2000, *Participating in God: A Pastoral Doctrine of the Trinity*, London: Darton, Longman and Todd, p. 52.

midst of the local, for others it means a redirection of vision. For all there is a practice of 'triple listening', listening to God, to each other and to the culture. In 2 Corinthians the apostle Paul writes of God's mission of reconciliation and challenges us to be ambassadors of reconciliation. This is the work of the Trinity, restoring community and relationships into the body. Paul continues that God's reconciliation is based in grace, not counting sins but promising new life. For new monastic communities the desire to take the message of reconciliation into the midst of culture while resisting the temptation to use the tools of power is critical. The words of the prophet Micah, 'to act justly and to love mercy and to walk humbly with your God', challenge us to stand for others, to relinquish our own rights and to trust daily and deeply in God's leading. This shapes the way many new monastic communities engage with the people they meet in the towns and cities in which they live.

During the struggles for democracy in South Korea a movement known as 'Sharing House' emerged. It grew as student priests involved in the democracy campaigns began to bring together their theological studies with their concern for justice and community. There are now around 70 Sharing House communities in South Korea, who live and work, among others, with children, abused women, orphans, migrant workers and the homeless. These communities are in their own way new monastic communities. They teach languages and skills, start social enterprises to provide work, offer counselling, shelter and, most of all, love. Each Sharing House is led by an Anglican priest who leads worship for the people of the community around them. Revd Kim Hong-Il, one of the founders of the movement, said:

We are concerned with healing and releasing the poor from the instability of unemployment and irregular employment. We joined with the people who protest against forced displacement and work to build low-rent public apartments, and helped them to achieve community autonomy. We fought poverty with them. We participated in education through daycare centres and literacy classes and practised holistic care for the sick.

Korean society is multireligious. Therefore we pursue our own version of a church community, living together to fit into our local conditions. Christianity is inseparable from community.[8]

New monasticism combines a desire for a deeper relationship with God, a deeper relationship with each other and a deeper relationship with the world into which God leads us. As we seek to be community enveloped within the community which is the Trinity so we encounter God in fresh ways. We meet God in the midst of God's ongoing life. So worship and prayer are about joining in with God, and mission is about catching up with what God is already doing as God seeks to restore all things into right relationship with God.

The image of the church that resonates most closely with its trinitarian foundation would most likely be that of the people of God. The church community, participating in God's life, is God's special people, a people living God's life of communion in a covenant of relation and love.[9]

Developing accountability in community

Direction is not a matter of command and control, but of focusing, allowing and encouraging people to focus on what really matters. It is spiritual management rather than micro-management. Leadership is about contaminating and being contaminated with knowledge. The distinction between learning, working and living is gone – it is one and the same thing.[10]

One of the questions most often asked of new monastic communities is, 'How are you accountable?' While it may be true that this can be a loaded question, born in fear and suspicion,

8 In conversation with Mark Berry in Seoul, 2012.

9 S. B. Bevans and R. P. Schroeder, 2004, *Constants in Context: A Theology of Mission for Today*, Maryknoll, NY: Orbis Books, p. 299.

10 Kjell Nordstrom and Jonas Ridderstrale, 2000, *Funky Business*, Ontario: Pearson Education, p. 215.

it is nevertheless a valid one. New monastic communities do not exist in a vacuum, in fact the overwhelming majority, as explored elsewhere in this book, have a deep sense of their connectedness to the long history and deep traditions of Christian community and spirituality. The desire to reflect the nature of the Trinity also compels new monastics to want to develop a relationship of mutual learning and support with the wider Church. At the same time, many have a challenging relationship with the structures of the Church today. So, how do we build good and generous relationships which allow others to ask us difficult questions? How do we give due and humble respect to the traditions and leadership of God's Church? How do we find practices that ensure the safety and well-being of our communities and those whom we serve? How do we model peace and reconciliation at home as well as abroad?

There are no simple answers to the above questions; individual new monastic communities have developed different practices and relationships within their own context and story. Indeed for some, questions of accountability are a very real struggle, whereas for others there are naturally emerging solutions. For all there is a degree of 'creative tension', held by a real sense of the need to be part of something bigger, to learn from others and to be held to account for who and what we are.

During its time as part of the Diocese of Lichfield, safespace held a regular day with a group including the local bishop, leaders from the Church Mission Society and invited others, often including a visitor from a traditional monastic community. The day began with a time of meditation and prayer led by the community, introducing themes and practices which were current for the community and its mission. The community would then spend the morning talking about what had happened since the last gathering and what issues were currently at play. After eating lunch together the afternoon was always a time for discussion led by the rural dean and the day ended with prayer for the ongoing life of the community. This practice, alongside more frequent formal meetings with the rural dean, gave the community real opportunity to wrestle with its community practice, spirituality and calling and for it to be challenged by others. For safespace it has always been important for those who hold them accountable to regularly participate in the life of the community, to join them at table, in life and in worship, to see the community in action.

For safespace, the relationship with CMS has become important to ground the community in the long history and experience of mission which shaped CMS. It has been vital for safespace to have wise and reflective people walking alongside, sometimes participating, sometimes questioning, always challenging.

The Moot community is a good example of a new monastic community working within Church of England diocesan and deanery structures. As its main home is currently the Guild Church of St Mary Aldermary in the City of London, it falls under the jurisdiction of the Archdeaconry of London. In so doing it has a priest in charge and a Guild Church Council. However Moot has been intentional in ensuring that the community retains its new monastic basis. The Moot Community therefore has accountability to the Archdeacon of London, and the bishop who oversees the Two Cities areas of the Diocese of London. Moot therefore has a deanery synod representative who is elected from the community and the priest in charge is a member of the City deanery.

Regarding governance, Moot has a monthly community council, which functions as the Guild Church council, where any participant in the community who has affirmed elements of the community's rhythm of life can raise issues. This council ensures that it listens carefully to the opinions and concerns of all its members.

Within its new monastic structures, Moot has a standing committee to oversee the daily running of its office and staff, and two pastors who work collaboratively with the priest to oversee pastoral accountability and the welfare of the whole community. To sustain its new monastic basis, Moot has a written constitution that defines not only its rhythm of life but also how governance and accountability are sustained. In its structure as a dispersed community are 'Mini-Moots' which are regular gatherings of a few mooters around food, prayer and study. These operate as spaces of individual accountability for people to be supported and grow regarding living the elements of the rhythm of life and expected spiritual practices. In addition to this Moot is influenced by two external visitors, Abbot Stuart of the Anglican Benedictines and Sister Joyce of the Anglican Franciscans, concerning how the community develops its new monastic life. As will be discussed later, the Bishop of London has given permission for the body that oversees Religious Communities in the Church of England to discern whether Moot is ready to launch what it desires as a New Monastic Acknowledged Religious Community. This process is seeking permission and accountability to grow Moot so that it can operate in different places in and outside the Diocese of London. Finally Moot makes it explicit that all participants of its life are expected to have an external spiritual director to help them grow in faith and spirituality and, importantly, accountability.

Community life

When told how wonderful it must be to live in community and asked what it means on a daily basis an abbot of a trad-itional monastic community replied, 'It means that when one of my brothers comes to ask me about a missing kitchen knife, I tell him to go and look in the backs of his brothers!' We must resist the temptation to romanticize community; it is not easy. It has great strengths, but it also has great challenges. We are all human beings and we all have our 'moments'. Perhaps the great-est struggle for us as we build community is to manage our egos and our interpersonal interactions. Living, as we do, in a culture that is foundationally individualistic many of us have lost or not acquired the skills we need to be in community. So community itself is a place of learning about community.

The mayBe community in Oxford, England say about them-selves, 'We are realistic about community. It's not always easy. But we are committed to the idea of authentic community and, more importantly, to enabling authentic community to happen in and around us in mayBe ... We are cultivating generosity. We are practising forgiveness. We honour each other.' This is no easy

commitment to make and the word 'practising' carries two mean-
ings; to do it and to seek to perfect it. To grow healthy community
requires a truly honest struggle with what it means to be me, what
it means to be human and with our own reactions to others. St
Benedict challenges the monks to 'practise this zeal with most
ardent love; namely, that in honour they forerun one another.
Let them bear their infirmities, whether of body or mind, with the
utmost patience.'[11] How do we 'deal' with challenges that relationships bring? How do we hold on to community when there is
argument and anger? How do we cope with people who seek to
dominate and include those who lack confidence? The first thing
we need to do is be observant, to make ourselves aware of what is
happening in our communities on a daily basis; to identify where
people clash, where storms are brewing and to talk openly and
honestly with and about each other. This does not mean that we
seek to avoid or eradicate conflict; conflict is a normal and healthy
part of community life. We need to properly embrace conflict
while 'practising forgiveness' and grow robust mechanisms for
restitution; ways in which members can say sorry with honesty
and dignity. Shakespeare wrote in *The Merchant of Venice*:

> The quality of mercy is not strained.
> It droppeth as the gentle rain from heaven
> Upon the place beneath ...
> It is an attribute to God himself.
> And earthly power doth then show likest God's
> When mercy seasons justice.[12]

Just as the nature of God is held in the interconnections between
the Trinity, so maintaining the health of our communities requires
nurturing the space between people as well as the people themselves.

The ancient monastic communities we refer to as Celtic developed a praxis called 'anam cara' (sometimes spelled 'anam
chara'), meaning 'soul friend'. Michael Mitton, writer and former

---

11 Rule of St Benedict, Chapter 72 trans. Boniface Verheyen OSB (1949).
12 Shakespeare, *The Merchant of Venice*, Act 4, Scene 1.

member of the leadership of Acorn Christian Healing Founda-tion[13] and Christian Listeners says that the concept of the Soul Friend grew in the desert communities as a kind of spiritual guide for reflection and as a counsellor. In both the early desert and the later European communities these soul friends were a crucial part of both the individual personal searching and the structure of the community.[14]

In our culture we are scared of this level of openness and vulnerability, and in some ways rightly so. It must be approached with real consideration and care. We fear letting others know our innermost insecurities and struggles, we do not want to give any-one power over us. Many of us have been hurt, used and abused by others in whom we have in the past put our trust. Indeed, in his book, *Anam Cara: Spiritual Wisdom from the Celtic World*, John O'Donohue, Irish poet, author and priest, warns:

Here you need deep prayer, great vigilance and care in order to redirect your souls. Love can hurt us deeply. We need to take great care. The blade of nothingness cuts deeply. Others want to love, to give themselves, but they have no energy. They carry around in their hearts the corpses of past relationships, addicted to hurt as confirmation of identity. Where a friendship recognizes itself as a gift, it will remain open to its own ground of blessing. When you love, you open your life to an Other. All barriers are down. Your protective distances collapse. This person is given absolute permission to come into the deepest temple of your spirit.[15]

He goes on to say that this deep level of relationship is 'an act of recognition and belonging'; in other words it is how we dis-cover who we are and how we connect. We are human because we belong. We participate. We share.

---

13 As recorded at http://www.acornchristian.org.

14 Michael Mitton, 1995, *Restoring the Woven Cord: Strands of Celtic Christianity for the Church Today*, London: Darton, Longman and Todd.

15 John O'Donohue, 1997, *Anam Cara: Spiritual Wisdom from the Celtic World*, London: Bantam, p. 34.

It is often a feature of new monastic communities that children are not separated from the life of the community and indeed often participate fully. Stanley Grenz, American Baptist theologian and ethicist, writes on the role of the Holy Spirit in drawing the community together as one family in God.

> Participation in the dynamic of Trinitarian love, however, is not ours merely as individuals in isolation. Rather, it is a privilege we share with all other believers. Because of Christ's work on our behalf and the Spirit's activity within us we are co-adoptees into the family of God, co-participants in the relationship enjoyed between the Father and the Son, which is the Holy Spirit. In mediating this relationship to us the Spirit draws us together as one family. Only in our Spirit-produced corporateness do we truly reflect to all creation the grand dynamic that lies at the heart of the triune God.[16]

The life of a new monastic community is deeply rooted in this belief and experience of God as community. The struggles we face with each other and with others emerge from a realization that we do not exist in a vacuum and therefore cannot hide from each other, from God or from the world around us.

So for new monastic communities it is critical that this level of relationship and intimacy is facilitated and nurtured, but it also has to be recognized that it carries risks. Many new monastic communities deliberately live their lives with people who are wounded and hurting. For some this means growing community with others who suffer mental illness, depression or broken relationships, and this needs holding with care and attention. Alongside the need to live with the challenges of the everyday ordinary struggle we all face as individuals, a majority of new monastic communities in Britain contain families. Living like this in close proximity and relationship with children and vulnerable people brings its own complexities and dangers. Therefore recognizing and nurturing

---

16 Stanley Grenz, 1994, *Theology for the Community of God*, Nashville: Broadman and Holman, p. 484.

relationships that provide a deep level of accountability are critical in keeping the community healthy.

While we can only experience an imperfect echo of the community of God, community is our created nature. Therefore, if we recognize its challenges and properly embrace the difficulties it will be a creative and dynamic existence which speaks to the heart of our culture about the very nature of God.

We walk together in peace
Clearing all misunderstandings
Forgiving all wrongs
Confessing all prejudice
Discarding all stereotypes
Sacrificing all pride
Learning to love
Learning to walk together
Learning to see beyond experience
Learning to look forward
Learning to be
In God is community
In God there can be community
In God we are enfolded in community
In God we learn community
In God we model community
We pray together for peace
Global peace and local peace[17]

17 A liturgy written and used by safespace at The Table, the weekly gathering of the safespace community.

PART 2

Intentionally Prayerful and Spiritual

4

Living a Rhythm of Life

Community is about sharing our lives with each other. It speaks of a common way of living in which certain priorities may be reckoned as important or foundational. It does not necessarily involve living together on a day-to-day basis. A rule of community describes and outlines a way for living adhered to by its companions.[1]

What new monastics describe as a rhythm of life draws on the traditional monastic rules, but goes further in that it seeks to be a holistic and all-embracing approach to opening up a healthy approach to the spiritual life in community. A rhythm of life seeks to answer the question 'How do we live in our context but not of it?' Most of all it is a guide, hopefully to inspire, an aspiration seeking to affirm what is good concerning contemporary society, but also seeking to be countercultural to the overly individualistic, materialistic and consumptive cultural norms.[2]

To do this effectively, a rhythm of life needs to cover three areas of life:

- **BODY** (Orthopathy) – **Right feeling and being**
  Well-being and healthy approaches that do not neglect physical and psychological needs.

---

1 Introduction to the Northumbria Community Rhythm of Life, http://www.northumbriacommunity.org/who-we-are/journeying-with-the-community (accessed 21 October 2009).

2 I understand that some will be concerned that such an approach will involve 'dumbing-down' of the tradition. We sincerely do not believe this to be true; more of a different approach to contextual theology and mission.

- SPIRIT (Orthopraxis) – **Right living and action**
  Behaviour, spiritual practices and healthy living.
- MIND (Orthodoxy) – **Right thinking and knowing**
  Wisdom, knowledge, understanding, study and healthy thinking.

In new monasticism, there are many variant ways that a rhythm of life has been drawn together. However, there are four main themes and structures that seem to be emerging:

1. Aspirations – entry or explorer level of commitments for those who can belong but not necessarily believe.
2. Virtues and Spiritual Practices – defining what it means to be a new monastic Christian. For some there are additional practices expected of those who are given room to exercise particular vocations of service.
3. Postures – defining a way of living a life of Christian worship and openness to God in the ordinary and everyday.
4. Ethos – the theological and philosophical thinking, understanding or foundations of this form of ecclesial community.

Aspirations

Aspirations open up the beginning of a rhythm of life seeking to answer the question, *How should we live?* and focuses on living out values as a pattern for life. In effect a rhythm of life is a set of statements owned by a community to encourage a pattern of lifestyle, a rhythm of living. For traditional monastics and mendicants, this is about a commitment to prayer and seeking the love of God and sharing it out with others, believing this to be the central call of discipleship, of the kingdom of God on earth.

The great gift of a rhythm of life is that it directly engages with people's existential yearnings and longings about the question, *How can I live healthily and justly?* For the Northumbria Community, this was about engaging with the question inspired by biblical texts:

Who is it that you seek?
How then shall we live?
How shall we sing the Lord's song in a strange land?[3]

The Northumbria Community has two key elements to the Aspirational level of their rhythm of life: *availability* and *vulnerability*.

> **Availability** to God and to others expressed in a commitment to being alone with God in the cell of our own heart; it involves not only solitude but hospitality, intercession and mission ... it also involves an intentional **Vulnerability** expressed through being teachable in the discipline of prayer; the wisdom of the Scriptures and mutual accountability in the advocacy of soul friends ... being receptive to constructive criticism; affirming that relationship matters more than reputation and living openly among people as Church without walls.[4]

Such a focus then is about radical hospitality, and the seeking to be fully human. The Moot community took a similar approach in their construction of a rhythm of life, but asked a different question which yielded a slightly different result:

> How should we live in but not of contemporary culture and our busy City of London. How should we live? We seek to affirm all that is good, but also question what is unjust and dehumanises.[5]

Their rhythm of life directly seeks to answer this question with aspirational statements of intention to live *in* but not *of* contemporary culture:

presence
We commit to journeying together with God and each other, by meeting together as a community, in prayer, in worship,

---

3 Northumbria Community Rhythm of Life.
4 Northumbria Community Rhythm of Life.
5 http://www.moot.uk.net/blog/about/rhythm-of-life (accessed 10 April 2007).

friendship, grief, and happiness. Being a hopeful sign of an open community in the city rather than just a group of individuals or anonymous people.

acceptance

We desire to accept both ourselves and other people as they are, and to allow people to say what they believe without fear of judgment. We want to create a safe space where people feel at home and welcomed. We hope to learn from all those in and outside the community.

creativity

We want to have an open approach to how we learn, live and encounter God in the plurality of our city and the world. We wish to be creative in our worship, in prayer, in our lives, in learning, and with the Christian tradition, in our theology and with the arts.

balance

We aspire to live with integrity in the city, striving as a community for balance between work, rest and play. We wish to develop healthy spiritual disciplines such as daily prayer, meditation and contemplation, drawing on the ancient Christian paths. We want to live within our means, living sustainable lives. We desire to be not simply consumers, but people committed to giving and receiving in all of life.

accountability

Within the rhythm of life we desire to be accountable to one another, to grow and journey together, listening to each other and the wider Christian community for wisdom rather than trusting only ourselves. We want to have a willingness to share life, rather than to privatise it and we seek to walk together in a deep way rather than as strangers who only know the surface of each other.

hospitality
We wish to welcome all whom we encounter, when we are gathered and when we are dispersed, extending Christ's gracious invitation to relationship, meaning and life in all its fullness.[6]

The Moot approach to a rhythm of life then is a whole-of-life venture, a radical call to discipleship or praxis for a community as well as for individuals.

Here then is the first great advantage: the Aspirations assist a contemporary rhythm of life to be used in such a way that acknowledges we all have uniquely different personalities, interests and vocations. It then enables people to explore an interpretation of the rhythm of life that enables them to continue on their own particular spiritual pilgrimage, while finding depth with others who are also interpreting such a rhythm of life in their own lives. The Aspirations define a community that is on a pilgrimage together, except this pilgrimage has the potential to last the rest of life, as it is fundamentally about seeking God, growing in Christian faith and, as a result, becoming more human.

Taking this approach, the Aspirations of a rhythm of life enable new monastic communities to have fluid edges (that is, easy to join in, enabling people to 'belong before believing'), but at the same time does not dumb down on the faith through having a deeply Christ-centred heart of a community defined by the Virtues and Spiritual Practices. In this way, a rhythm of life creates a rare dynamic: an accessible faith and community of praxis along with a deep connection to a Christian interpretation of a way of living. This double dynamic allows for missional expressions of new monastic communities, opening up the Christian faith as a deep resource that has a great deal to say about what it means to be spiritual and human in the twenty-first century.

The 24–7 Boiler Room communities have three elements to their principles (equivalent to the Aspirations of a rhythm of life). At the heart of every Boiler Room is a living community committed to being:

---

6 Mark McCleary, Ian Mobsby, Carey Radcliffe and Michael L. Radcliffe (eds), 2009, *Moot Little and Compline Services, Pocket Liturgies*, London: Proost.

1. Authentic: true to Christ
2. Relational: kind to people
3. Missional: taking the gospel to the world.[7]

There is a playfulness in many new monastic communities as they seek to follow the Jesus of the Gospels who munched, talked and partied with all sorts of seekers and outsiders. New monastics are rediscovering that you can do church and life, have fun and live passionately. Aspirations are a powerful tool for building community, mission and evangelism through the way new monastics seek to live.

Setting these Aspirations to reflect God's calling in a particular context is not an easy task. Different communities have different stories, some where the bar was set too low, when Christian faith is in danger of being undersold, or the struggle of the Christian life is not acknowledged fully or taken seriously; or the reverse, where the bar is set too high and the rhythm of life makes the Christian life burdensome and unsustainable. Getting the Aspirations and the Spiritual Practices right is important. One of the core commitments to a rhythm of life is to regularly reaffirm your commitment to it publicly before an identified external person or persons. New monastic communities that have a relationship with a particular denomination or tradition need to explore how this accountability can be done in conversation with governance structures. For many this could be before a bishop, archdeacon, superintendent, or equivalent ecclesial leader. The Moot community reaffirms its commitment before the Bishop of London every Easter, and the mayBe community in Oxford has recommitted to their rhythm of life before an Anglican suffragan (assisting) bishop.

Virtues

Virtues are an attempt to counteract the thoughts that distort us (sins) by a disciplined approach to the thoughts that give us life (virtues). This relates to the ancient idea of 'deadly sins'. In a

7 Andy Freeman and Pete Greig, 2007, *Punk Monk*, Ventura, CA: Regal, p. 235.

culture which is obsessed with outer freedom and neglects inner discipline, many people in contemporary culture are held captive to their inner compulsions and addictions, and such distorting cravings and obsessions can feel quite literally like controlling external demons. As Abbot Jamison said:

> The Eight Thoughts have the potential to damage our well-being, they throw us off balance and lead us away from happiness. They come from within us and yet sometimes they seem to be bigger than we are and so they are described as attacking us from without. Contemporary meanings of happiness mainly involve feeling good, with the emphasis on feeling. Contemplation involves knowing the good, the sense of knowing here being like that of knowing a friend rather than knowing a fact. Virtue involves doing good, as in living out the virtues.[8]

The Moot community has summarized virtues and sins as follows:[9]

	Virtues	Sins
About the body	Moderation (*sobriety*) Chaste Love (*innocence*) Generosity (*non-attachment*)	Gluttony (*intemperance*) Lust (*shamelessness*) Greed (*avarice*)
About heart and mind	Patience (*serenity*) Gladness Courage Spiritual Awareness	Anger (*impatience*) Sadness Fear (*anxiety*) Spiritual Carelessness
About the human spirit	Magnanimity Humility Honesty (*truthfulness*)	Vanity Pride Deceit (*untruth*)

As we explored earlier, many monastics put great store in the development of humility as a key aspect of being a monastic or

---

8 Christopher Jamison, 2009, *Finding Happiness*, London: Phoenix, pp. 22, 42.

9 Aaron Kennedy and Ian Mobsby, *The Rhythm of Life: Virtues, Postures and Practices, A Proposal to the Moot Community*, 10, http://www.moot.uk.net/community/community-discussion-forum/ (accessed 30 April 2010).

mendicant. For Benedict, humility was specifically tied into discipleship. This was inspired by the Beatitudes, that great teaching of
Christ in the Sermon on the Mount.[10] In practice this means that
living out a daily rhythm of life and its associated practices should
lead to changes in who we are, through the transformative love of
God. Quite literally by seeking inner freedom from the thoughts
that distort us to inhabit thoughts that give us life. People become
more fully present to themselves and God's love, which should
bring increased peace, tolerance and love in how adherents to
this way of life relate to others. For many new monastics such as
the Northumbria Community these Virtues are expressed in the
values and practices of the community. Other communities, such
as COTA, have formulated virtues as well:

- generosity, living abundantly
- graciousness, living with grace
- thankfulness, being a priest, living Eucharist[11]
- humility, the ability to be honest and to learn
- accountability, the ability to be responsible for what you do
  before God and others
- compassion, the ability to walk beside
- transformation, the capacity to change and grow
- obedience, the ability to follow and listen
- courage, the capacity to move through fear
- faith, the capacity to trust God
- hope, the capacity to move forward
- love, the capacity to give yourself away.[12]

There is something very healthy about encouraging people to
become more human, and to that end the virtues of humility and
gentleness are important.

---

10 See Matthew chapter 5.

11 This community and most new monastics have a high view of the 'priesthood
of all believers'.

12 Karen Ward, *Life Together in the Way of Jesus. A Rule of Life for Church
of the Apostles, Seattle,* http://docs.google.com/View?id=dgxt8gcs_37hnkk46hc
(accessed 23 October 2009).

Spiritual Practices

The Spiritual Practices seek to name what it means to be a committed follower of Jesus Christ in the context of a spiritual community. They seek to express the vocation to worship, mission and community for individuals and for the community. Again in practice they need to reflect how often dispersed participants live this out in different ways reflecting variations in personality, life situation and vocation. Many new monastic communities suggest that each participant has an external spiritual director to assist them develop their understandings of the rhythm of life so that they live it fully. Moot state a desire that those in the community develop a form of daily and weekly prayer, but they are careful to allow room for people to use different forms of prayer, meditation and contemplation to encounter God in ways that are meaningful given the variance of personality type and lifestyle. Moot's spiritual practices are:

- The practice of **prayer and meditation** (daily, rhythmic, individual and in community)
- The practice of **mercy and justice** (personally, locally and globally)
- The practice and **facilitation of communal worship** (contemplative, Eucharist, Compline, etc.)
- The practice of **learning** (discussions, biblical reflection, reading, spiritual direction and retreats)
- The practice of **presence** (making an effort to develop and maintain deep relationships with those in the community and to tithe financially as regular giving)
- The practice of **mission** (assisting people to explore and experience Christian spirituality, being a soul friend to those in and outside the community)
- The practice of **passionate living** (living life to the full, but also the passion of sharing in God's suffering for the world).

The rhythm of life of the Contemplative Fire community has two elements (*travelling light* and *dwelling deep*) with three areas of focus within this:

- Encountering the present moment in quietness
- Engaging with wisdom on the boundaries
- Equipping, exploring and accompanying others.[13]

The Church of the Apostles in Seattle has been very explicit in their spiritual practices, critiquing and reframing some of the expectations of traditional monastics:

- weekly eucharist
- daily office
- scripture reflection
- hospitality
- discernment
- tithing
- confession
- forgiveness
- fasting
- feasting
- retreat
- pilgrimage.[14]

The 24–7 Boiler Rooms have also taken a high view of developing six spiritual practices to underpin their three principles. These are summarised as:

1. The practice of **Prayer** (daily, rhythmic, individual and in community)
2. The practice of **Mission** (both outreach and inreach)
3. The practice of **Mercy and Justice** (personally, locally and globally)
4. The practice of **Hospitality and Pilgrimage**
5. The practice of **Creativity**
6. The practice of **Learning and Discipleship**.[15]

---

13 Contemplative Fire rhythm of life, http://www.contemplativefire.org/guide.htm (accessed 23 October 2009).

14 Ward, *Life Together*.

15 Freeman and Greig, *Punk Monk*, pp. 237–8 (my emphasis).

The great gift that 24–7 Boiler Rooms has developed is the twin process of spiritual practices enabling an inward journey of spiritual formation and the outward journey of social transformation and mission. This has enabled 24–7 Boiler Rooms to be effective, radical and deep expressions of missional community with younger people.

Lessons can be learned from the new monastic communities that set the bar around Spiritual Practices too high. One community known to the authors gave members the option to make vows each Easter, for a set of spiritual disciplines. This group, a sub-group of the whole community, would become a chapter, where the ordained priest became an abbot, and where the chapter elected a prior to support the abbot and assist in the pastoral support of the chapter. These spiritual practices were inspired by taking aspects of traditional monasticism and reframing them. One of these practices was the commitment to pray at midday every day stopping whatever you were doing, to join in the chapter which, however dispersed, stopped to pray. As time went on, fewer and fewer of the community were willing to commit to the rhythm of life and the associated expected practices.

This example raises a number of issues. First, when formulating a rhythm of life in a new monastic context, it is important that this is managed in a 'bottom-up' way. Time needs to be taken into account in establishing and instigating a rhythm of life to ensure it is widely owned.

The second issue in this example is the danger of setting up a 'two-speed' community, with an instituted inner circle existing in and on top of a wider circle. Clearly, all communities have different spaces of belonging and commitment, but great care needs to be taken to prevent exclusion. In traditional monastic communities, there are different levels of belonging, again with a chapter for those who have taken life vows, and with a group of novices who do not join chapter meetings until they have taken vows. It is the view of the authors that in a new monastic context such a structure may erode the great gift of being one committed community giving and learning from each other, as a created hierarchy of belonging does not include everyone in the community.

Great care needs to be taken to maintain the advantages of an open new monastic community for mission and ministry, which could be undone in such a model.

The Moot community has experimented with the idea of 'spaces of belonging' rather than 'levels of belonging'. This then gives room for people to be in different stages of faith but where the focus on being one community in terms of participation and belonging is retained. This also recognizes that those on the spiritual journey are on a dynamic and not a linear journey, where there are times of orientation to disorientation. The diagram below illustrates how within Moot it is possible for people to go through periods of faith and doubt and remain part of the one spiritual community.

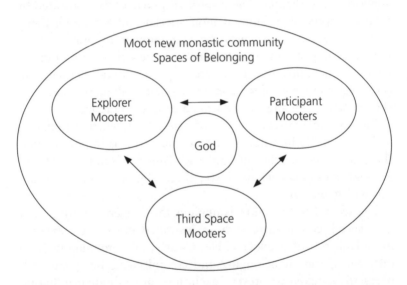

Thinking again about the context of a culture addicted to consumption, spiritual practices may be incorporated to draw on the deep gift of the contemplative tradition which resonates strongly with the focus of meeting God inside as well as outside in the world. Contemplation and meditation are forms of prayer to be nurtured and developed which bring consolation and encounter with God. Among spiritual practices, one might consider contemplative forms of prayer as well as a balance of work, rest and play as expressions of different aspects of the Christian life.

Postures

Postures, as the word suggests, relate the meaning of movement with spiritual encounter (from which we get 'prayer postures'). Postures are therefore a disposition of openness to encounter God through any aspect of life by being attentive to this possibility. Such postures then become possible from a combined commitment to a rhythm of life, spiritual practices and virtues. If you ever get the chance to see a Carthusian monk at prayer, you will notice these postures lived out in a very radical way. Every aspect of life is quite literally a medium to encounter the divine.

While virtues are an expression of attitude and expressed interpersonally with other people, postures are an expression of attitude focused on our transcendent relationship to and with God (the 'I–Thou' relationship). Again, a few communities have defined their interpretation of this, but the COTA offers a very clear direction.

- Presence
- Openness
- Mindfulness
- Expectancy
- Wonder.[16]

The one great advantage of this approach is that it gives direction to explorers and participants who will hopefully grow into becoming new Christians, through an explicit focus on postures to assist contemplation, prayer and meditation.

Postures also provide an explicit anchor concerning the qualities of a healthy spiritual life for those who have been Christian for a while. It is a marvellous door, enabling people to explore the contemplative and mystical Christian traditions – essential

16 Ward, *Life Together*.

if Christianity is to find a contextual place in the twenty-first century.

Living it frees the Spirit

From a rhythm of life of Aspirations, Spiritual Practice, Virtues and Postures develops a basis of encounter with God and others in the world. Naming this is essential if a rhythm of life is going to be life-giving. Both Miroslav Volf and Jemma Allen have written about a successful, participative life:

> A participative model of church requires more than just values and practices that correspond to participative institutions. The church is not first of all a realm of moral purposes; it is the anticipation, constituted by the presence of the Spirit of God, of the eschatological gathering of the entire people of God in communion with the triune God. Hence the church needs the vivifying presence of the Spirit, and without this presence, even a church with a decentralised participative structure and culture will become sterile, and perhaps more sterile even than a hierarchical church. For it will either have to operate with more subtle or open forms of coercion. Successful participative church life must be sustained by deep spirituality. Only the person who lives from the Spirit of communion (2 Cor. 13.13) can participate authentically in the life of the ecclesial community.[17]

> Friendship is not some gimmick that we can market as a way of successfully living a Christian life. It is not even primarily about an act of will or making friendships in a calculating way. Friendship as a spiritual practice, as the mark of a disciple, as a proclamation of the Good News of the Reign of God – this friendship is about entering into authentic relationships of vulnerability and trust, relationships of mutuality and care.

17 Miroslav Volf, 1998, *After Our Likeness: The Church as the Image of the Trinity*, Grand Rapids, MI: Eerdmans, p. 257.

In allowing ourselves to be affected by who we live with and how we live with them, by the gifts we receive in and from our friends, we open ourselves to being transformed by love and so enlarging the realm of God: the kinship and new community proclaimed by Christ. That, my friends, would be Good News![18]

Development of a spiritual life resourced in and with the Holy Spirit is essential if new monasticism and its focus on a rhythm of life are going to work. Human beings find life in community resourced by the source of all life, the Spirit of life in God.

---

18 Jemma Allen, *Homily at the Moot Community Eucharist on 11 October 2009*, http://mootuk.podbean.com/2009/10/11/christ-friend-god-and-the-kin-dom/.

5

Forming a Rhythm of Life

At the heart of a rhythm of life is the desire to know and to follow Christ wherever you are ... simplicity is the key, the rhythms of life that have worked, and continue to work are those that are easily understood and grasped, this does not mean they are simplistic. The simplicity means that it is far easier to work them into everyday life, as they are easy to memorise. Most rhythms can be reduced to just a few words, behind which lie the core ideas and hopes of the community.[1]

As we have said, the formation process right from its outset cannot be rushed, and needs to utilize a 'bottom-up' communal approach. If it is to be deeply owned, it requires the investment of the whole community. There are a number of different approaches to developing a rhythm of life, and the communities that utilized a more inclusive developmental process seem to own their rhythm of life more than attempts to impose it through a 'top-down' system.

The process outlined below has been used by the Moot community and a number of other new monastic groups and has worked well as a 'bottom-up' approach. This assumes that a community is less than 160 people and is ideally suited for communities up to 100.

If your community is greater than 160 people, we suggest you break down a number of parallel working groups to reflect the membership of the community, where each of these working groups has no more than 60 people. In such a situation you will need to take much more time to complete the process if it

---

1 Gareth Powell, 'Developing a Rhythm of Life' in Mark McCleary, Ian Mobsby, Carey Radcliffe and Michael L. Radcliffe (eds), 2009, *Moot Little and Compline Services, Pocket Liturgies*, London: Proost.

is going to be representative of the community's life, values and spirituality.

First things

A good starting place begins with awareness and discernment. Your community will want to get into a rhythm of meeting at least monthly about this. Explore the beginnings of the early church in the Gospels and the Acts of the Apostles. Ask the question, *What can we learn from these early communities?* as a community in the twenty-first century. The discussion coming out of these interactions is crucial as people begin to name their aspirations and hopes. By naming and listening to individual aspirations, the story of your community begins to emerge. It may be helpful for you to meet and dialogue with other new monastic communities, and draw on their experiences.

Beginning by naming the aspirations

Spend a day exploring the question, *What are you passionate about concerning this community, why is it important to you, and what is God seeking for it to become?* Asking this question is deliberately incarnational. This approach assumes that God, the Spirit of life, is already stirring and unsettling members of your community with hopes and visions about what could be. By exploring this question, you are seeking to hear what God is saying to people directly. So on this day, invite everyone in your community, from those who have been around from the beginning right up to people who have recently become involved.

For the first part of the day, invite those involved from the beginning to have a few minutes to answer the question above, and continue up to the most recent member of the community. It is important that the community be attentive to every person's story. While each person speaks, it is vital that someone else keeps track, writing down the key words that were used. As you build up the content from a number of stories you will see that natural groupings begin to emerge.

To do this well, you may wish to project these words and short sentences up on a screen using a computer tablet or write on acetate for an overhead projector. The community is normally extremely engaged with this process because it has come from them.

Then invite the community to explore how they could group the words and short sentences into specific areas, and then give each of these groups a single word name to cover the variant elements contained within it. At the end of the day, explain that the process had been about discerning what God was doing through the lives of people, and that you have been listening not just to individuals of the community, but to God speaking through the community. Explain that now the community needs to meet regularly to start developing a rhythm of life out of the identified key areas to answer the question about what God is calling your community to be, and to answer the question, *How should we live in but not of the contemporary world?*

Following through the process in this way, the rhythm of life will be deeply owned, because it was crafted out of the lives of those involved in your community, and driven by the Spirit of God. Remind people, though, it may take some time to get it right, so be careful with your process, not to formulate it too quickly or without adequate consultation. The process took the Moot community a whole year to complete.

Plan for the Development Day

1. Welcome
2. Prayer
3. Listening to the voices of the community from the founders to the newest people. Someone writes down words and phrases visibly for the community to see
4. Group words in up to nine categories or groupings
5. Give single words as titles to the groups

6. Explain the process for developing a rhythm of life, and the plan for the regular meeting to shape the groupings into elements
7. Concluding prayer

Completing the Aspirations – first post-development day meeting

Allow at least a couple of weeks to pass between rhythm of life development meetings, to allow people to reflect on what has been written and articulated. The next series of meetings are aimed at developing the groupings and their one-word headings (created in the development day) into aspirational statements of the community focusing on *how we should live in but not of contemporary culture* and what God is unsettling and thereby envisioning your community to be. Through this process, the groupings become shaped into elements of your evolving rhythm of life. You will need at least one meeting of two to three hours to look at one grouping and its heading. At this stage, where people are now interested, it may be a good idea to look at what other new monastics have developed, but absolutely avoid copying what they have done.

For this process of meetings, invite up to two people from your community (given adequate time to reflect) to explore the particular group and heading you are focusing on, and what it means for them and what they think God may be saying regarding a calling and aspiration for the community. Invite them to share their thoughts in this process for around six to eight minutes each. Ensure that you use two different people at each meeting, aiming to include the whole community at some stage of the development if possible.

Once the groupings have been discussed and explored, the next stage of each meeting is the most difficult: writing an aspirational statement. This will require discussion. You will need someone to facilitate or chair each of these meetings to ensure that everyone gathered can have a say, and that the proceedings are not overly dominated by a few outspoken members.

Beginning statements with 'we' and 'we aspire to ...' is a good starting place to try and find a common language for the particular element of the rhythm of life. Discussions may point towards a more appropriate word for naming the element, so be careful not to be overly defensive of a word if the community would like to see it changed. The aspirational element should affirm some form of intention that critiques or challenges some area of life. For example, affirming generosity and hospitality while challenging injustice and exclusion.[2]

Sometimes this is an easy task when there is clear consensus in the community, and much harder when there are very different views on the element you are looking at. Where there are differing voices, this will need time for the conversation to shift from the aspirations of individuals to becoming the story and aspiration of a community, so healthy discussion is a must. Try to get as much wording down as you can where there is consensus. Remember, the more straightforward the language, the easier it will be to be owned. Keeping it simple is the key.

Whatever else, the element of the rhythm of life needs to be inspirational as well as aspirational, so if it ends up sounding like aims and objectives, then you will need to put in more work, as the passion of the community must be contained within the wording. If you get stuck, and it becomes obvious that complete consensus over the whole wording for the element is not yet possible or clear, do not force it. Write down what you have been able to agree upon, and return to it later, and move on to another grouping in the next meeting.

Further gatherings of the community

It is crucial to maintain momentum in writing the rhythm of life, so with meeting monthly it can take up to a year to develop a rhythm of life. For some communities this is fast enough, but meeting twice monthly may reduce time if your community is working well. Most communities will end up with five to eight elements of

2 See example elements of the different rhythms of life listed in Chapter 4.

a rhythm of life, so if you have more than nine, you may need to think whether all of these are viable. In this case, it may be that you have combined elements of a rhythm of life with virtues and postures. Again, use your community to work out which are the key elements – note that nine is a maximum number.

You may wish to look at the previous chapter to see what other communities have done to divide up their elements of a rhythm of life from virtues and postures. So this phase of development needs to continue until you have drafts for each element of the evolving rhythm of life, using the approach and principles stated above. Below is a reminder and summary of the plan for these meetings:

1. Welcome
2. Prayer
3. Reminder of what you as a community are forming with a rhythm of life
4. Facilitator to introduce element to be discussed, the title and the wording grouped in it
5. Person 1 to share their reflections for six to eight minutes
6. Person 2 to share their reflections for six to eight minutes
7. Discussion and group work to reshape the grouping into an aspirational statement
8. Agree a final wording for the element
9. Where consensus is not reached, write down what you have been able to achieve and where you have got stuck
10. Remind people of the next meeting and which two members of your community are sharing in the process
11. Concluding prayer

Refinement phase

Once you have drafted as many of the aspirational elements as you can, you will need to go back to the elements where consensus for a definitive statement had not been reached. Again, commit one meeting to each element. Try to find a wording that reflects the factors that people in the community want to see present. You may want to give space for people to express the different perspectives, and for the community to find some form of middle way. Given that so much has been achieved so far, there will be peer pressure to finish what has been started, which helps find solutions.

We have not yet heard of a community that – through sticking at it – did not find consensus. If you really cannot, then you may be forced to take a majority vote on a solution, but this is less than ideal. Once you have drafted the aspirations of the rhythm of life with one-word headings and aspirational descriptions, consider a time for reflection and refinement. There may be crucial elements that have been missed: for example, do the elements of your rhythm of life ensure a balance of worship, mission and community? If not, then you may need to adjust your rhythm of life. Elements that relate to mission need to be outward-focused, or else they are not really mission. This may require further exploration and adaptation.

When the Moot community went through this process, a number of people were concerned about the under-representation of the need for outward-looking mission. In the monthly meeting process, they revisited three elements of the rhythm of life, changing some of the wording to ensure a better balance. The hOME community in Oxford also went through a similar refinement process, as they too, on reflection, felt that mission was initially understated in their rhythm of life. Given that this has happened to a number of communities, we would stress the importance of ensuring a healthy balance between worship, mission and community, if your group is going to reflect a healthy expression of Christian ecclesial community.

You may want to send out the aspirations section of the rhythm of life in written form to each member of your community for final reflection and have a meeting to celebrate it, when consensus is reached. Remember, development could go on forever, so making an informed ending to the process is important, but note that the community may want to review this in a few years' time. The experience of other new monastic communities indicates that you should fully write up the aspirations of the rhythm of life and some form of introduction, so that new people can understand and own the community's rhythm of life story.[3] Once established, do not review the rhythm of life for a while, as the next stage needs to consider the associated spiritual practices, virtues and postures. Here is a summary of this stage as a reminder:

1. Gather together all that has been agreed, and go back to the elements where agreement was not possible to seek consensus
2. If consensus is not possible, take a majority vote
3. Allow for a time of reflection
4. Ensure there is a balance between worship, mission and community. Often outward mission is under-represented. If this is so, reflect on what elements could be strengthened to ensure better balance
5. Compile a final draft with single word headings and aspirational descriptions
6. Give out copies to the community
7. Celebrate its creation, and make a formal ending of the process
8. Recommit to reviewing the rhythm of life in a couple of years' time
9. Write an introduction to the rhythm of life so that new people can understand what it is for and why you created it. Tell the story of your community

Embedding the Aspirations of your rhythm of life into the DNA of your community

One key way to allow the rhythm of life to fully engage in the DNA of your community is to use an annual renewal of commitment service. It is the practice of monastics and priests in Holy Week to reaffirm their commitment to their vows. Continuing with this tradition, many new monastics reaffirm their commitment to their rhythm of life by a special reaffirmation service normally before an abbot or bishop. Moot, hOME and mayBE have all

---

3 For an example of this, see the Moot community introduction, downloadable from the Moot blog, http://www.mootblog.net.

playfully incorporated traditional monastic affirmations to their vows, reframing these liturgies into something more akin to alternative worship (for example, an alternative Eucharist) with the bishop presiding. For Moot, making these commitments to the aspirations of its rhythm of life is what makes you a participant of the community. If your community is not in relationship with a denomination with bishops, seek out the support of an equivalent senior minister. If you are in an independent new monastic community, then one option may be to foster a relationship with a local traditional monastic or friar community. Having such a relationship with a Franciscan, Benedictine or other monastic community may be mutually beneficial and promote cross-context learning. New monastics come from a very wide range of church traditions, and we have been encouraged by the interest and support of abbots, Franciscan provincial ministers and mothers superior for new monastic communities.

Another good way of getting the rhythm of life into the DNA of your community is to allow the seasons of Epiphany and Lent to form a monthly theme relating to elements of the rhythm of life. For example, in 2010 Moot used the theme of *presence* in January, *acceptance* in February and *accountability* in March. Moot's monthly programme of discussions, worship services and explorations then enabled the community to go deep with its rhythm of life.

If the rhythm of life is going to enter the DNA of your community, you should ensure that it is accessible, and that it is always included when your community tells its story to visitors, the wider Church and new people. It needs to be visible. A number of communities ensure this by making it prominent on all their public presences including websites, flyers and other publicity.

A key area has to be the commitment to opening up the rhythm of life for new people to the community. It cannot be expected that they should just accept it with little understanding. Moot organize occasional meals where different members of the community tell the story of the community and the place of the rhythm of life, and give people the opportunity to ask questions about its purpose and application. In this way, the rhythm of life can become a deep resource to inform the life and activities of the new monastic community. None of us will ever arrive at fully achieving the aspirations of the rhythm of life. We should never be able to tick off a rhythm of life as something we have achieved. The fruits of it will help us grow into an ever-maturing expression of faith.

Spiritual practices

If the rhythm of life of a community is going to bring a deeply resourcing spirituality, developing the spiritual practices associated with the rhythm of life is crucial. Many new monastic communities have developed a use of various forms of the contemplative Christian tradition to help grow this sense of spiritual depth. While later in this book we will specifically explore different forms of contemplative prayer that can assist in this development, initially we would suggest inviting the community to experiment and explore different forms of ancient prayers reframed for contemporary life and practice. The impetus is to encourage people to explore ways to incorporate different forms of prayer into their own personal spiritual rhythms, which, it is hoped, will bring lasting spiritual nourishment.

Whatever else you do, avoid rushing into a formalized list of expected spiritual practices until the community has had a real chance to develop its contemplative prayer life. As we said earlier, the quickest way of killing a rhythm of life is to set the bar concerning spiritual practices too high. Set the bar deliberately low, with an invitational approach to develop spiritual disciplines through exposing people to different forms of prayer, and leave it till later before formalizing the practices.

When it comes to the setting of spiritual disciplines, we would recommend developing a balance between each member's personal spiritual life and the community coming together in regular worship and involvement in outward focused action.

Listed below are areas that new monastic communities might include. We suggest you use this to begin a discussion about spiritual practices, when you think your community is ready.

1. Meditation – the regular practice of silence utilizing a John Main or a 'centring prayer' approach with the repetition of an anchor or holy word as a focus.
2. Prayer and contemplation – the regular rhythm of differing forms of prayer such as Ignatian meditation, imaginative prayer or the examen, where such prayer is understood as encounter with God, or joining in prayer with God the Trinity.
3. Engagement with Scripture – a commitment for your story to be informed and immersed in the story of God and the people of God through spiritual practices such as *Lectio Divina*, and study as critical exploration of texts.
4. Eucharist – a commitment to participate and receive Holy Communion.
5. Confession – a commitment to face your shadow-self, to knowing yourself deeply and making time to face the things that you do wrong, and to grow in the process. Having a spiritual director or soul friend is an expected part of accountability and also of developing spiritual maturity.
6. Tithing – a commitment to share a proportion of your regular income with your community.
7. Mission – a commitment to making time for involvement in giving action to the world.
8. Hospitality or action – to give time in support of those less fortunate than yourself; giving friendship and love to those who face serious social or other kinds of deprivation. God can speak to us through everyone we meet, and particularly those who are poor and marginalized.
9. Retreat – a commitment to spending time away from life for your own well-being as well as to spend time with God in prayer.
10. Daily Office – a commitment to pray Morning and Evening Prayer elements. Some communities such as the Northumbria Community have developed their own liturgies for Morning and Evening Prayer, whereas other communities merely commit to Morning Prayer.
11. Turn taking – a commitment to be involved in leading the worship, mission and life of the community.

Avoid the use of controlling language that makes unreasonable expectations, and keep things broad so that people can develop their own spiritual rhythm within the context of the spiritual rhythms of the community. You will find that this facilitatory approach will disarm resistance and actually promote a spirit of inquisitiveness, remembering that these are not rules, but an attempt to provide a guide to developing and sustaining a healthy spiritual life.

Also use a consultative approach to the formation of spiritual practices, asking the question, *What spiritual practices bring us life already, and what do we need to develop?* and again allow group responses. The above list of spiritual practices came out of a consultation completed with a new monastic community using such a process. It is crucial to make sure that the spiritual practices are clearly distinct and different from the language of your Aspirations, or it will get very confusing. For example, don't use the words 'practice of presence' for both an Aspiration and a Spiritual Practice. You might find it helpful to invite members of other new monastic communities with formalized spiritual practices to be in dialogue with your community in order to help it synthesize important elements for your community's spiritual life.

Virtues

Once you have established spiritual practices and a rhythm of life, you will want to consider virtues. Not all new monastics have a formalized set of virtues, but we would recommend that your community consider it. You may want to just affirm the virtues and sins as documented in the previous chapter, which we believe to be robust. Understanding the 'thoughts that distort' and the 'thoughts that give you life' is very important. Churches often assume that being able to 'do-and-be' community is a given. Some new monastic communities have realized that many people who have grown up in an overly individualistic and consumptive culture are not skilled in interpersonal skills, let alone a commitment to the giving and showing of love. Further, the way we interact with others has much to do with the health of our own inner life. The way we treat others comes from the way we treat ourselves.

New monastic communities need to be explicit about a set of expected 'practices-as-virtues' regarding what it means to be loving in relationships with people. In this way, we enable people to grow and change and in effect become more human through a whole-of-life approach to discipleship. Having virtues names some of the expected interpersonal practices as we seek to grow in discipleship and see the world as interacting with the kingdom of God. This is not to say that a community should avoid disagreement and difficult issues by always trying to be nice to each other. Instead, having virtues gives you the ground rules and spiritual basis for respectful interpersonal relationships that then encourages trust and openness to promote maturity so that disagreements and issues can be faced and managed well.

Humility and empathy (and not false humility, which is a form of indirect aggression) are about becoming a people of peace, where individuals can reach beyond their own ego and narcissism to see the world as it really is, and loving friendships as the loci of the kingdom of God. A good place to start developing virtues for your community would be to explore the qualities that Jesus practised in the Gospels, and deciding the aspects that are important for your community to imitate. This would encompass a study on the Beatitudes; how this important scriptural passage names qualities that come out of developing the Christian spiritual life. Another approach would be to ask the question, *Of the people you know, who would you say was the most authentic Christian or spiritual person, and what qualities does she or he have that makes you think this way?*

Postures

As with virtues, not many new monastic communities have formalized Postures. This section explores the sensibilities that enable a healthy and sustaining spiritual life, through a dynamic spiritual and mystical relationship with the Triune God. This is possibly the hardest to conceive and complete, but it is nonetheless crucial. In the twenty-first century, the Church is struggling to articulate the faith and open up contextually authentic approaches to discipleship/catechesis, so Postures is an aid for those wanting to explore through experience.

The word Postures also implies that the spiritual life is something that has to be worked at, and not just consumed, and that the outcome is not about consumer ego-related gratification, but the mystery of encountering the divine which is absence just as much as it is presence. Postures need to inform the struggle and difficulties of Christian spirituality alongside the joy of encountering the divine. You will have noticed that the language in this section has become more metaphorical – this lies at the heart of postures. Postures require you to overcome the incessant need to be in control, to always be in your head, or always driven by the outcome of your personal emotions. Postures encourage us to step back from our narcissistic preoccupations, and to be open to the playfulness and source of all love in the universe. After all, prayer and worship in the Christian tradition is about joining in with the Holy Trinity. This is essentially why Christian spirituality is so different to every other esoteric spirituality and religion, in that it is deeply and paradoxically relational and mystical.

To develop a set of Postures requires maturity, and it may take a while for a community to get to this point. We would suggest that a new monastic community appoint a working group of people interested in this area, and who have the maturity and motivation to help shape these slowly and carefully. So a process of forming a working group, in dialogue with other new monastics who have Postures, and in dialogue with traditional monastics, allows for formation of Postures more fully. Then, when the time is right, you can present a draft document about this to the whole community (depending on your governance system).

6

Encountering God through the Contemplative and Sacramental

The Christian of the future will be a mystic or he or she will not exist at all.[1]

Those forms of spirituality in the West that help people to live in accordance with the deepest, sacred dimension of their own unique lives can be expected to be growing.[2]

In previous chapters we explored the importance of knowing God as a spiritual encounter rather than an intellectual approach of knowing God through facts. This is not saying that facts and the narrative of the Christian faith are not important. It rather admits that in a consumptive society, encounter of God is a vital focus. As with all things, this is not new. You could look at Abraham and the apostle Paul as examples of this *experience-leading-to-understanding* approach to discipleship and faith formation. It is also possible to look to the example of St Francis of Assisi, for in his life it was experience that led to understanding. For example, he experienced the Holy Trinity not as some intellectual construct, but as a living truth to be experienced and encountered through daily prayer.

It is therefore no coincidence that there is a current and resurgent interest in the ancient resources of the Christian faith regarding prayer and spiritual practices. The need for ecclesial communities to be enthusiastic facilitators of spiritual disciplines

---

1 Karl Rahner, 1981, *Theological Investigations Vol 20, Concern for the Church*, London: Darton, Longman and Todd, p. 149.

2 P. Heelas et al., 2004, *Spiritual Revolution*, 7, Oxford: Wiley-Blackwell.

is vital if Christianity is to be seen to have anything to offer in the twenty-first century. As Drane and Taylor have said:

> It is ironic, to say the least, that the church is in serious decline exactly at the same time as our whole culture is experiencing a rising tide of spiritual concern – and that many of today's spiritual searchers dismiss the church, not because it is irrelevant or old-fashioned, but because in their minds it is 'unspiritual'.[3]

> This [change in culture] is being reflected in the wider Christian culture in the rise of such things as the concept of Ancient–Future Worship, the interest in Monasticism, and the practice of spiritual disciplines.[4]

For new monastics seeking to develop an increasingly contemplative approach to prayer and meditation, this begins with the concept of *monos* – the need to be with God. For some people this can feel counter-intuitive and also threatening. In our culture, saturated with information technology, entertainment and busyness, just being alone, still and quiet can feel hugely unsettling. An excellent place to start involves finding a good mentor, spiritual director or soul friend to assist you to deepen your spiritual life. Each of these different approaches seeks to support and encourage the individual to go deeper. One of the greatest problems in being still, alone and quiet is that you have to face yourself. This can be a deeply painful first step, as emotions, aspirations, disappointments and frustrations with one's journey of life suddenly become a focus rather than left in the subconscious. Some may need substantive pastoral support to face this stage, even beginning with some counselling. Being able to face *monos* is an important first step.

In a beautiful illustration, Teresa of Ávila, a monastic and mystic, described the development of a spiritual life through a

3 John Drane, 2000, *Cultural Change and Biblical Faith: The Future of the Church. Biblical and Missiological Essays for the New Century*, Carlisle: Paternoster Press, p. 76.
4 Barry Taylor, 2008, *Entertainment Theology*, Grand Rapids, MI: Baker Academic, p. 182.

pattern of spiritual disciplines, akin to building your own silk-worm cocoon. As the silk worm is committed to a daily pattern of sustenance and the creation of silk to build a cocoon as a home, so God, by the grace of God's Holy Spirit, finds a home in us through our regular practice of prayerful presence. So as the silkworm is transformed by the cocoon from something not altogether attractive into a butterfly, seemingly dying then finding new life, so we, through committed prayerful encounter of the divine through meditation, contemplation and daily prayer, can enable the Holy Spirit to dwell in us and change us, through the love of God. Teresa said this to her fellow nuns:

> This shows, my daughters, how much, by God's grace, we can do, by preparing this home for ourselves, towards making God our dwelling-place as God is in the prayer of union. You will suppose that I mean we can take away from or add something to God when I say that God is our home, and that we can make this home and dwell in it by our own power. Indeed we can: though we can neither deprive God of anything nor add to God, yet we can take away from and add to ourselves, like the silkworms. The little we can do will hardly have been accomplished when this insignificant work of ours, which amounts to nothing at all, will be united by God in divine greatness and thus enhanced with such immense value that our God will be the reward of our toil. Although God has had the greatest share in it, God will join our trifling pains to the bitter sufferings the Redeemer endured for us and make them one. Forward then, my daughters! hasten over your work and build the little cocoon.[5]

The aim of this form of prayer is not only encounter with God, but realising that meditation and prayer are about joining in with the persons of the Trinity who are in a constantly prayerful relationship, which we, through the grace of God, are invited to join. This prayer – this cocoon – this place of growth – also points to

5 From Chapter 2 of *The Interior Castle*, by St Teresa of Ávila, taken from http://www.ccel.org/ccel/teresa/castle2.ix.ii.html on 2/8/13.

the vision and ultimate destiny of a Christian, to develop a deep relationship with and to God. So deep that we increasingly will be relationally inseparable from the loving God.

Meditation

Meditation as a spiritual discipline in the Christian tradition is all about seeking to be still, getting beyond our own thinking and feeling, in order to encounter God. There are many approaches to meditation. We have found two approaches particularly helpful, and both have to be learned and practised regularly. In teaching and explaining these with your community, rather than expecting people just to 'get it', all new monastic communities should explore the need to run regular group meditation sessions to enable people to learn and practise particular approaches. The Moot community currently runs a weekly meditation group to support people in Moot develop personal meditation, as well as open up the Christian contemplative tradition to stressed city workers. Both approaches have a three-point focus:

1. Finding stillness.
2. Getting beyond one's thinking and feeling.
3. Encountering God.

The first group of meditations uses a sacred word to be thought repetitively. Some use the ancient phrase *Jesus Christ, Son of God, have mercy on me, a sinner*. Others use the phrase broken down into *Mar–an–a–tha*; others use the ancient Jewish breath prayer broken down into two breathed phrases, *Yah–weh*, the first breathed in, the second breathed out repeatedly.[6]

In the first phase, stillness is achieved by sitting upright in a chair, with eyes closed and with controlled breathing. When thoughts come into your head, this approach suggests you acknowledge

---

6 To explore this more fully see the 'World Community for Christian Meditation' developed by John Main, or 'Contemplative Action' developed by the Franciscan Friar Richard Rohr, https://cac.org/.

them and then let them go. This can be quite a battle, and some-times it is just not possible to find stillness, and this is okay. Equally, sounds may distract, but again you acknowledge these and let them go. Stillness is about quietening the ongoing chatter that goes on in our head and the avoidance of distraction, to then be able to seek God. This can be helped by prerecording some relaxing music, fading it to silence, timing the silence for 20 or 25 minutes, and then fading the music back in with rising volume.

In the second phase, this approach to meditation encourages the participant to acknowledge feelings, emotions and thoughts, and then to let them go, using the repetitive phrase as an anchor to keep focus. Again, it can be difficult to get beyond thinking and feeling, and all you can do is find stillness using the anchor phrase to assist you to maintain this stage. However, with practice, there will be increasing times when you can get beyond your thinking and feeling as moments then to experience and encounter God. This final stage is always fleeting, and never long sustained.

Some approaches in this first group of meditations allow the participant to focus on a flame or to imagine repetitive dripping water when unable to focus on the repeated word. For those just starting out, it is suggested that a 20-minute meditation is attempted, progressing to 25 minutes of meditation when it feels right. Groups such as the John Main World Community of Meditation suggest that individual meditation should be practised daily.

The group meditation that the Moot community uses each week is largely:

1. Welcome
2. Reminder about good posture in sitting and removal of shoes
3. Physical relaxation technique for ten minutes
4. Introduction to the sacred repetitive word approach and the three stages of meditation
5. Prerecorded music to silence or a bell – and 20 or 25 minutes of meditation using the sacred word
6. Short wisdom reading on meditation or a Christian mystic or contemplative

7. Short, open questions or discussion on what was experienced or discovered in the session
8. Closing prayer of blessing.

To aid personal meditation at home, you may find it helpful to create a spiritual space. For example, Ian, in his small shared flat in London, has a chair bought specifically for prayer and meditation.

> I only sit in it and light a candle when I am attempting to pray and meditate. I have found this ritualistic approach has helped me focus better. I aim to meditate three times a week – once at the group meditation, and twice at home. I do not always achieve this, but it is good to see this as an aspiration rather than feeling it is a mark that must be attained and then feeling guilty when it does not happen.

If you do not find meditation rewarding to your spiritual life, you are unlikely to want to keep going, so it is important not to have too high an expectation of yourself during this phase to avoid it becoming a potential source of guilt.

One myth worth immediately quashing is the idea that meditation is for introverts, and that extroverts need something more engaging of people and activity. As extroverts, both of us have found meditation deeply important. It can help one face the real 'me', to expose the shadows and delusions of one's own ego, and to encounter God who seeks to enable one to become more human. This is not only time for 'me', but a form of prayer that helps one grow. Whether or not to meditate is not about introvert versus extrovert. Meditation enables us to face who we really are, and then encounter God away from our own issues, ego, masks, inflated emotions and delusions.

In our experience and that of our communities, those who are unable to engage in silence and meditation often need to entertain themselves and keep busy, because they have deep underlying issues they need to face. Where people are struggling with the consequences of modern society – addiction, emotional neglect and on occasion abuse – being still is very difficult. Such situations need to be handled sensitively and skilfully. Yet, if you do not know who you really are, then meditation is very tough. This is often because people are too much in their heads, and somewhat emotionally immature. The wonder of the last stage of meditation, encountering God, is that this can be deeply beautiful and transformative. In the Christian tradition this 'I–Thou' relationship is where we gain a personal understanding of the self, not only by knowing ourselves and knowing who we are through the feedback of friends. This form of meditation results in our personal identities being informed by God in mystical encounter.

The second grouping of Christian meditation uses a different approach to the idea of a repetitive word or phrase. It is loosely more about 'abiding'. You can do this at home, by the sea, simply standing in the wind, or where there is some form of repetitive noise. In this abiding approach, being present to where you are is the focus where the repetitive noise becomes the anchor. For the more visual, using a candle or a dripping tap, or running water can be the anchor. For some, being by the sea, using the anchor of waves, is extremely enriching. In this approach, the focus remains the three stages discussed earlier, but where the anchor is an external rather than an internal locus. Alternating these two approaches in different parts of your weekly rhythm of life can be beneficial.

In the meditation group run by the Moot community, participants report the benefit of meditation in their wider lives, sensing God's presence or a sense of inner peace, or deep connection with God. Meditation not only helps to reduce stress and promote relaxation, it also enables people to become more spiritually aware and attentive to God's prompting in the ordinariness of life, whether it be at work, an emotional response to something read, or the words used in an encounter with a street beggar. The regular practice of meditation helps the participant to become more aware of the promptings of the Holy Spirit, and thereby become a mystic. So meditation is a really important tool in the spiritual disciplines.

Contemplation

Where meditation is about stillness and getting beyond your thinking and feeling, contemplation is about actively using thinking and feeling for creative encounter with God. The focus here is on creativity and the imagination, in the belief that part of prayer is about God the Holy Spirit encountering us through our creative imaginations, through personal encounter in the I–Thou relationship. This approach can be tremendously liberating and exciting but again, mature expressions of contemplation come out of committed practice and space in our lives. The focus is on encountering God in life, where life itself becomes a spiritual quest: 'Life is a sacred adventure. Every day we encounter signs that point to the active presence of Spirit in the world around us.'[7]

> The achievement of divine simplicity implies not the annihilation of the complex world but its illumination and transfiguration, its integration in a higher unity. This will involve the appearance of a new type of saint who will take upon himself the burden of the complex world.[8]

Contemplation, therefore, is an important discipline, opening up the spiritual landscape of God's activity in the details of our lives. God is speaking to us through the medium of our every day, but all too often we are not aware of this presence. This spiritual sensitivity needs to be developed. It is through contemplation that we enter into an adventure, attempting to discern and catch up with God through an attentive approach to prayer, which does not fear the complexity of the world, but drives us into it. To meditate is to quest after God, and there are a number of different approaches that can deeply resource the spiritual life. These we will now explore.

---

7 Taylor, *Entertainment Theology*, p. 86.
8 Nicholas Berdyaev, 1939, *Spirit and Reality*, London: G. Bless, p. 98.

The examen

The examen is a particular approach to contemplative prayer, which seeks to find God in the details of your daily life, in moments of consolation and at times of desolation. The monastic founder of the Society of Jesus, or the Jesuits, St Ignatius of Loyola, developed this approach to prayer to assist people to seek God's guidance in life, and to further an increased awareness of God's presence.

To explore this type of prayer regularly, you may want to make notes or to journal to assist in remembering the insights gained from this form of contemplative prayer. Below is a basic framework:

1. Reserve some quiet time and space on a weekly basis, in a place where you will not be disturbed or distracted. Lighting a candle can remind you that this is a form of prayer, where you are seeking God's presence.
2. Reflect on a moment in your day or week when you felt most grateful, that moment when you felt most alive. When were you most able to give and receive love in this situation? What could God be communicating to you through this event or happening?
3. Reflect on a moment in your day or week when you felt least grateful – when you were least able to give and receive love – when you felt angry, drained or lifeless. Try to be honest before God as you recall what was said and done in that moment which made it so difficult. What could this situation reveal to you about God and God's love for you?
4. Finally, do not form any judgements about yourself or others, but simply give thanks for both situations, and seek God's love to support and sustain you just as you are. After a time of silent prayer, seeking to receive from God, write some notes to help you remember the detail of the outcome of this prayer, to help you dig deeper to know yourself and seek God's guidance in your life.

Ignatian contemplative prayer

Like the examen, Ignatian contemplative prayer was developed by St Ignatius as an important spiritual discipline. In Ignatian contemplation, you are encouraged to use your creative imagination to place yourself in a particular biblical story and situation, so that you can experience the situation for yourself. All the senses are invoked – taste, touch, smell, hearing and sight – to fully explore and enter the situation. Some approaches to this form of prayer invite creative encounters with God in and through the stories.

The Gospels are full of situations and stories fitting for Ignatian contemplative prayer, for an encounter. Again, it requires discipline to begin this prayerful exploration in a place where you are not going to be distracted.

Ian tells of a time when he was very low and went on a retreat with daily spiritual direction from one of the residents at the convent. This approach proved a life-saver, and for him the creative experiences around the story of the road to Emmaus became a rich resource for encountering God. As a result he wrote a liturgy, his own take on an Ignatian contemplative prayer around the Gospel story of the road to Emmaus.

It is a hot day, you can taste the heat of a new day. You are walking, quickly, away from the city of Jerusalem. You walk silently with two other friends of yours, disciples of the Jesus who has died. You can hear the breathing of your friends, and the footsteps against the mud road. You remember your sadness, that this Jesus who had brought such hope and joy was now gone. You feel that deep sense of fear and sadness.

You look ahead, and see a figure wearing a cloak over his head, who is standing watching you approach him. One of your colleagues asks him directly, 'What do you want?'

He responds in a quiet voice, 'May I join you on your journey?' Everybody nods and the strange figure joins you.

After a few minutes, the figure asks you where you are going, and why you seem so sad. You answer, 'Have you not seen or heard the terrible news of today, the things that have gone on in Jerusalem in the last days?'

One of your friends continues, 'They have killed Jesus of Nazareth, of whom we had great hope that he would be the Messiah.' For a few minutes there is no sound other than footsteps and rhythmic breathing.

Then the strange figure asks, 'So why are you sad; were not these things foretold?' He then goes through the Scriptures beginning with the Hebrew books of the Law, exploring the texts about the Messiah and the will of God. He knows his stuff, so much that he talks about this for over an hour while walking. It is encouraging to hear him talk so authoritatively about the events that have happened. I can tell by the conversations that I am not the only one to be encouraged. We talk all day!

In your mind's eye, what do you see, what do you feel? [Pause]

Well, as we approach the small village of Emmaus, the evening is beginning to draw in, and I can see the house we are to reside in. So one of the friends asks the stranger to join us for the evening to continue our discussions, and eat with us. The stranger agrees.

So we gather in the house, and I address this stranger. Now that I can see this stranger's face, he looks tired.

What do you see, what do you feel? [Pause]

You want to say something to him – this compassionate stranger – what do you say? [Pause]

What does this stranger say to you? [Pause]

We come into the kitchen to the smell of cooking food and bread. We sit down at the table, and continue talking.

What do you see, what do you feel? [Pause]

We ask the stranger to bless us and the meal before we start. The figure stands up, says a blessing and breaks bread. And it is then in those words we realize that this is Jesus, this is the Messiah, and then he disappears.

We all stand up in shock, all of us realize at the same time, that this was Jesus. We are all shocked!

What do you see, what do you feel? [Pause]

You remember the look on Jesus' face as he looked into your eyes before he disappeared.

What did his face look like? [Pause]

What was Jesus communicating to you?

This approach to creative contemplation is very powerful, and can be used in individual and group prayer times. Not only does this help people dig deeper in their self-understanding, but opens up the importance of reflection and wonder, to seek God in life. This form of prayer really helps people to learn to appreciate themselves, and to explore how God connects with people as unique expressions of being human.

Lectio Divina

Lectio Divina is an ancient form of prayer that utilizes biblical texts as the focus for prayer and encounter with God. It means 'divine reading' and was created as a spiritual practice of prayer to promote communion with God. In its monastic form, it is usually used as part of daily Morning and Evening Prayer, using elements of the lectionary biblical passages. So it starts with Scripture and allows the participant to be drawn in and ultimately led to a place of rest and contemplation. There are four sections to this practice: *Lectio, Meditatio, Oratio, Contemplatio.* Below is a short approach to the core practice, which for monastics can last up to one hour.

Lectio – read
Read the Scripture passage once. It helps to read it aloud and softly. Get the general sense of the passage.

Meditatio – reflect and ruminate
Reading it again, let yourself begin to enter the passage: you may do this imaginatively, or you may like to just gently reflect on its meaning. Is there a passage, sentence or word that draws you? Let yourself be drawn. Begin to repeat that phrase, sentence or word over and over, allowing it to settle deeply in your heart. Relish the words; let them resound in your heart. Read the passage as often as you wish, learning these words by heart as you continue to repeat them in your mind. Let an attitude of quiet receptiveness permeate the prayer time, an openness to a deeper hearing of the Word of God.

Oratio – respond
As you continue to listen to/imagine the part of the passage you are drawn to, a prayer may arise spontaneously in response. Offer that prayer. What do you want to say to God/Jesus? What do you imagine God/Jesus wants to say to you?

Contemplatio – rest
Return to that part of the reflection so far that has moved you most deeply. Rest in the presence of God.

Contemplation on nature

One of the great inheritances of the Franciscan tradition is the openness to pray and encounter God through an aspect of nature. Francis of Assisi believed strongly that the divine presence of God can be encountered by close observation and love of nature. Below is a very simple approach to a Franciscan nature meditation.

1. Go outside into a natural environment. Seek out something that catches your eye which is of an organic nature – a leaf, tree, petal, blade of grass – something like that, something small.
2. Now really look at the object of your attention, look at its detail, encounter it, remaining silent and not distracted by anything else for about five minutes.
3. What do you like about the object of your attention, and how does it make you feel? Give yourself some time to reflect on this.
4. Do you feel anything that moves you about it? Does anything spark you to feel something in your spirit like awe or wonder? Give yourself time to reflect on this.
5. What does the object of your attention reveal about God? What does it reveal about the mystical connection with all living things? With the divine? Take time to explore this, continuing to look at the object of your attention.
6. As the reflection comes to an end, hold on to how it has made you think, made you feel, or brought meaning to you. You may find it helpful to write this down, or journal, to return to these insights at a later time.

Group contemplation

One practice which is halfway between imaginative prayer and *Lectio Divina* in a group setting is group contemplation. In this approach, you identify a phrase (mostly some form of biblical text) and then allow a group of people to creatively explore it. A good example is the Magnificat, the Song of Mary, found in Luke 1.46–55: 'My soul proclaims the greatness of the Lord, my spirit rejoices in God my saviour.' You begin by saying the phrase a number of times, and then saying one word, to which people say a word or a couple of words that comes to their mind as a form of wonderment. For example, the following words can be used in response to the opening phrase 'My soul': *Me, my essence, the spiritual me, the deep me, the me that is unique,* and so on. The great advantage of this approach is that it opens up known biblical phrases and allows people to re-engage with the spiritual meaning of a biblical passage, as a playful engagement with the Holy Spirit.

Godly play and wonderment

Godly play is a wonderful resource that has been developed from a more creative and mystical approach to prayer, and knowing God through experience. Originally it was designed as a form of religious education that follows the traditional lectionary calendar. Its use now has grown far and wide. It again is meant for a group setting, and enables adults and children to pray and wonder together. There are a number of manuals and training courses in the use of godly play. One version used reflects something of the style of Christ using biblical metaphorical and parabolic stories, enabling people to encounter God. An example is the story of Abraham and Sarah. You tell half the story and then pause, and then ask wonderment questions such as *I wonder what this story means? I wonder what is the most important part of the story? I wonder if there is a part of the story we can leave out?*

The storyteller then finishes the story. It can be an extremely exciting approach to use wonderment as a form of prayer, and I have seen adults profoundly moved by the insights of their children into aspects of spirituality.

Daily prayer

Having a daily and weekly rhythm to your spiritual life is very important. The Daily Office of Morning and Evening Prayer employs lectionary texts and reflections, but to be honest, this does not always allow room for much contemplative expression of prayer.

By inserting contemplation and meditation into daily prayer (like the ones listed), forms such as Anglican daily prayer can become accessible and spiritually nourishing for those seeking a more contemplative focus. It is advisable to miss out elements that are optional, to prevent prayer going on too long. New monastic groups such as Iona or the Northumbria Community have developed their own forms of daily prayer which we highly recommend exploring.

You can get creative in prayer even if you are very busy. For example listening to a guided contemplative prayer on CD or on your iPod on the way to work or doing a 15-minute meditation at a lunch or coffee break, you can absorb this sort of prayer practice into life if you want to. Remember that friars, nuns and monks normally completed hard labour for at least five to six hours a day as well! To commit to this requires us to face our need for a disciplined approach to prayer. In our consumptive culture, such discipline and commitment is extremely countercultural and requires effort. Finding extra time opens up space to experiment. Shane Claiborne comments, 'stop watching so much television, and suddenly you find loads of time to be more proactive'. So experiment with different forms of contemplative prayer as a weekly and daily rhythm of spirituality.

Many feel the need to include some forms of external stimuli for daily personal prayer and contemplation. There are a number of good podcasts you can utilize. The Moot community, for example, publishes two reflections a month (http://www.moot.uk.net) and safespace has used a series of images and poems. The Jesuits have a number of daily reflections, a mixture of readings, prayers and meditations. The World Community for Christian Meditation have published a number of podcasts about the John Main approach to meditation. Other new monastic groups including COTA in Seattle also have a good list of podcasts around the liturgical calendar (as well as contemporary chant music). The secret here is to give yourself permission to play in a committedly spiritual way.

Spiritual direction

It may seem counter-intuitive to many, but an external facilitator to encourage, challenge and support you as you explore a deeper spiritual life is an important resource. The need for spiritual direction from a wise soul friend is a very ancient monastic practice. Often we are blind to things that are very close to us, while others who get to know us well can see them more clearly.

There are now a number of validated courses in spiritual direction such as the Haden Institute in the USA or the London Centre for Spirituality. Most Anglican–Episcopal dioceses around the world, for instance, have a list of good spiritual director networks. Many are pastors and priests who offer spiritual direction at no cost. Some, tending to be therapists who also trained as spiritual directors, may charge by the hour.

Spiritual direction is, however, distinct from therapy, counselling or mentoring. It is particularly aimed at facilitating people to develop a healthy prayer and spiritual life, as well as assisting people to work out a balanced lifestyle. One of its important aims is to help people to explore subjective-life spiritual experiences through contemplative approaches to encountering God. In so doing, people learn more about themselves through the I–Thou relationship, that increases the participant's ability to grow in their humanity.

Growth in inner peace and humility are key signs of a growing Christian spiritual life, and spiritual direction can assist people to face their unhappiness and shadow sides, helping them to be more fulfilled by a deeply resourcing spiritual life. So as traditional Benedictine monks grow in their stages of humility to increased relationship with the divine under the instruction of their abbot, new monastics can grow in humility through ongoing spiritual direction. When you stop and try to be present both to yourself and to God, it can raise all sorts of emotional challenges. Many of us have used what are called 'maladaptive coping strategies' such as denial, flight or fight, retail therapy and the like, so it can be deeply painful to stop and face ourselves. Developing a contemplative approach to spiritual direction can begin in darkness, or as more mystical writers have said 'entering a cave', where you have to face your own demons, pains and doubts. Thus having a skilled spiritual director is very important for spiritual welfare. Spiritual direction can also help people to discern deeper issues requiring attention that may require counselling or other psychological support.

For Ian, spiritual direction has been a fundamentally important point of encouragement and solace.

My spiritual director is an Anglican Christian who is artistic, contemplative and a mystic. Her insights and encouragement have enabled me to sustain a spiritual life helping me face those parts of the self I dislike intensely, and has helped me cope when God has felt very absent, and when life has been tough. If I did not have a spiritual director, I am not sure my faith would be as deep, and certainly my own prayer life would, metaphorically speaking, look like a desert. At a particularly low point in my life, I went to a convent in southwest London for three days in silence in an attempt to engage with God when I felt deeply that I had been abandoned by God. There I received daily spiritual direction and partook in Ignatian meditation, the Daily Office, and Eucharist. I started out the retreat ragingly angry and hurt, with prayer rantings at God in the monastic garden. On the third day, Ignatian prayer enabled me to experience God in a wonderfully healing encounter, that restored my prayer and spiritual life. If it were not for my own spiritual director, as well as the spiritual director at that retreat, I am not sure I would have made it through the things that crowded in at me, like the weeds choking the seeds in the parable of the sower.

So, spiritual direction is a crucial element for new monastics to consider taking advantage of in order to develop a spiritual life, because there can be much darkness, pain and difficulty to this Christian journey through life.

Sacramental and new monastic

Holy Communion or the Eucharist (from the Greek word for 'thanksgiving') is an extremely important element of the worship life of most new monastic communities. The way this is done depends on the many different church traditions with which the particular new monastic community is associated. However, we have both found that it tends to be more participative and relational than in traditional forms of church, while retaining a focus on the mystical presence of Christ.

In the safespace community in Telford, Communion is central to its life and self-understanding as a missional community formed out of the presence of Christ, yet coming from a more 'low church' tradition:

> For a while we've been talking about the two-fold vitality of the communion meal for us (when we use the word vital, we mean both senses i.e. essential and life-giving) – vital in drawing and binding us as a communion/community before and with God/each other (a process in which we are adopted into a God who is community) and vital in drawing and binding us into mission (a process in which we are adopted into a God who is incarnate and dynamic), we talk about the communion as the life-blood of mission. This is something that has arisen for us from our experience as a community rather than some applied theos-knowledge. It is not a strategy we have adopted but a reality we have experienced. These experiences have moved us to fall in love with the Trinity in a new way, a way which now shapes our glimpses of God and our instinct for Church, the mutuality and the mystery, the love and the living, the forgiveness and the fruitfulness, the compassion and the connections.

The communion draws our eye to God incarnate and sacramental, to a sent God and a sacrificial God (was it any harder
for the Son to be separated from the Parent than it was for the
Parent to be separated from the Son?). A God who creates in
community, who redeems in community and who sustains in
community – source, word and breath. I guess then that it is
no surprise that we find ourselves deepest in God when we are
in community, when we find ourselves loving others, forgiving
others, seeing God in others, giving ourselves in surrender to
others and significantly breaking bread with others [we are one
body because we all share in one bread].[9]

In the Moot community in London, Anglican Common Worship
is followed, but the community has written their own Eucharistic
Prayer chants, where the celebrant sings the main prayer, and the
note is held by the community. At the Crossing New Monastic
Community, at Boston Episcopal Cathedral, most of the service
is orientated to 'call and response', making the liturgy very
participative, and where the various ritual movements of blessing are concelebrated by the whole community sharing in this
ritual action. Both the Moot and the Crossing made the liturgy
extremely powerful by its inclusive and participative liturgy. It
is clear to us that new monasticism is seeking to re-engage with
liturgy as the work of the people rather than a traditionalism that
can elevate clerical function to the level of magic.[10]

As with traditional monastics and mendicant communities,
ordained priesthood is but one expression of vocation, we do not
have hierarchical structures, but see ourselves as part of the priesthood of all believers.

Below are liturgical resources: a Moot contemplative worship
service, an agape Holy Communion, using the reserved sacrament, and a bread and wine safespace liturgy.

---

9 Taken from a safespace Community Internal Report 2011.

10 For a more in-depth look at liturgical practice of new monastic, emerging
church and fresh expressions of church, see Michael Perham and Mary Gray-Reeves,
2011, *The Hospitality of God: Emerging Worship for a Missional Church*, London:
SPCK.

Moot contemplative service

Welcome to the MOOT contemplative service. The evening begins with refreshments before going into a contemplative form of service that will last about one hour.

Invocation
We name the Triune God who brings hope and centredness to our world:
God the Creator, who brings all existence into being [light candle]
God the Redeemer, who brings us salvation showing us a better way to live, and who calls us to follow [light candle]
God the Companion, who sustains all life and enables us to grow and find wisdom [light candle]
God who is present to us now and always.

+ We meet in the name of the Creator, and of the Redeemer, and of the Companion. Amen.

Welcome
We welcome all to this place and this time to worship God.
All are welcome.
Find here acceptance, love and peace.
Encounter the divine. Relax, God is here.

Five minutes of disciplined silence

Introduction
Who is it that we worship?
We gather to worship the Lord our God.
How do we worship?
We worship you, O Lord,
with the whole of our minds
with all of our strength
and with all our being,
and to love our neighbour as ourselves.

May the prayers of our mouths
and the meditations of our hearts
be acceptable in your sight, O Lord.

Confession
Let us pause and remember this past week; as we do so, offering
it back to God, both the good and the bad.

Three minutes of disciplined silence

As we sit before you God, as a community modelling you, the
divine and perfect body, we are aware of our own individual
brokenness.

So easily we put ourselves before others. Too easily we allow our
emotions and pains to overtake us and hurt others. We use our
mouths and tongues given to build people up, to push people too
high or knock people too low. We have poisoned our planet, our
souls and our nations.

Lord, forgive us our selfishness,
Lord, forgive us.
Lord, forgive us our greed,
Lord, forgive us.
Lord, heal us from our brokenness,
Lord, heal us.
Lord, free us to be the human 'becomings' you call us to be,
Lord, restore us.

In a moment of silence we commit to you the things that we know
hold us back.
Let us affirm our faith trusting in God's love for us:

May our attitude be as that of Christ
Who being in very nature God, did not consider equality with
God something to be grasped, but made himself nothing, being in
the very nature of a servant, and became obedient to death, even
death on a tree.
Amen.

Meditation/contemplative prayer
Scripture and other readings
Storytelling/reflection
Responsive activity following reflection

Prayer
Let us pray for our community, and for the world.
Feel free to pray aloud or silently.
At the end of each prayer let us say
Lord in your mercy,
hear our prayer.

Time of prayer

We pray for all those known to us,
those for whom life is difficult and those who have difficult tasks
to face,
those who find it difficult being themselves,
those who have difficult people to work with or difficult situations
to work in,
those who live in fear, loneliness or in pain,
those who are ill, oppressed or poor.
Lord in your mercy, hear the prayers of your people. Amen.

End Liturgy
In this God, we find hope to envision us today and tomorrow.
In this God, we find life, sustenance and a future.
In this God, we join in with the whole of creation giving thanks
for all that is good.
In this God, we may struggle in life, but we will not be overcome.

As we leave this place and this time,
teach us to care for all that is entrusted to us.
Help us to share with others that which you have abundantly
given us.
Lead us to see what is possible when all seems impossible.
Enable us to stand up for justice when all seems to oppress.

Help us to love generously and to give unconditionally.
Give us hope and joy so that we can keep walking this Christian
road less travelled.
Teach us, help us, lead us, enable us, give us, love us.

Blessing
May we see and know God
in the world that's around us.
May God take us through desert
and take us through storms.
May God guide us, protect us,
and give us a purpose.
Lord, give us your peace
wherever you take us.
Bring us joyfully home,
Bring us joyfully home.
**+In the name of the Creator, and of the Redeemer, and of the
Companion. Amen.**

Moot simple agape Communion using reserved sacrament

*Agape, as compared to Eucharist, is more of a symbolic meal
focused on friendship. It relates to the ancient practice of table
fellowship. Accordingly, Moot has a high view of the symbolic
importance of this. Where possible, reserved sacrament is used for
the bread and wine for communion in the middle of the liturgy. So
this agape meal liturgy is used when the focus is on friendship.*[11]

Introduction: A meal for the spiritual journey
We have come together as friends, as companions on a shared
spiritual path. We are called to be a community of friends, to
journey with each other and God. To follow Jesus our God who
ate, drank, laughed and cried with people that he met – some with
much, and some with little. In this Jesus, we come face to face
with a God who desires our friendship; a triune God who loves

---

11 Reserved sacrament is used with the guidance of the Moot priest missioner.

us as the Creator, Redeemer and Companion; a God whose very nature is love, justice and friendship. Let us begin by being quiet and reflecting on this God: our God who died for our friendship, who is restoring our world, our relationship with each other and our relationship with God.

Silent pause

Readings
Reading 1 on the Passion
Luke 22.14–20

Reading 2 on the Passion and Crucifixion
John 13.34–36

Prayer
Let us, as friends, recommit ourselves to this co-journeying with God, recognizing our own faults and failings.

**God of Love,
we are sorry that we have acted and thought too highly of ourselves and others, and at times, too lowly of ourselves and others. Enable us to walk freely from our mistakes and failings on our journey of life with you. Only through your undeserved grace can we be free and call you friend.**

Reflective reading
Reflection from the book *Listening to Your Life* by Frederick Buechner, pp. 133–5.

Prayer
**God, we thank you that you have called us friends. We thank you, that in you we can find the source of life, our Creator, Redeemer and Companion.
We have a living hope as we, as companions, remember your life, free to follow you.
Christ has died, Christ is risen, Christ will come again.**

Reading
John 15.7–17

The meal
So let us celebrate and remember this friendship with God by
eating and drinking, and remember that we do this as spiritual
companions, the people of God. Food for the people of God.

Share the wine and bread

Open prayer
We have shared in our eating and drinking.
Let us now openly share our hopes and dreams with each other
before God –
for us as companions, this Church, our communities and the
world.

Allow time for open prayer

As our Redeemer has taught us, let us pray.
Our Father in heaven
Hallowed be your name.
Your Kingdom come,
Your will be done,
On earth as in heaven.
Give us this day our daily bread.
Forgive us our sins,
As we forgive those who sin against us.
And lead us not into temptation.
But deliver us from evil.
For the Kingdom, the power and
the glory are yours,
Now and forever.
Amen.

God, we thank you that you have drawn us together here as Moot,
in Central London, to be companions.

Help us to grow in our companionship.
Help us to be hospitable to others who come across us or join us.
Help us individually to grow in our 'human becoming', to be more like you.
Help us to be a community of spiritual friends committed to the path and enabling others to encounter you.
Bless and enable us we pray to be your disciples.

Let us share the grace of God.

**May the grace of our Lord Jesus Christ, the love of God,
and the fellowship of the Holy Spirit, keep us in eternal life, now and forever more. Amen.**

Bread and Wine safespace Liturgy

We know in faith that you hear and that all is in your hands. But still you taught us to pray and so we pray.

**Blessed One, our Father and our Mother
Holy is your name.
May your love be enacted in the world.
May your will be done
On earth as in heaven.
Give us today our daily bread
And forgive us our sins as we forgive those who sin against us.
Save us in the time of trial
and deliver us from evil.
For all that we do in your love,
and all that your love brings to birth,
and the fullness of love that will be
are yours, now and forever. Amen.**

Lectionary psalm

Lectionary Gospel

Quiet reflection and/or thoughts on the readings

Bread and wine

Community

We come as one, as family, as we draw together our prayers for the future and our hopes and fears. Welcome to the table, eating together is a vivid sign of community ... sharing tonight we are community, in communion with each other and with the creator and redeemer God. We reflect the image of a God who is by nature fellowship, family, yet family is difficult, it requires honesty and sacrifice ... it is vital that we are honest with each other and before God and that we give of ourselves to each other and to God's purpose.

Global

In sharing this meal we share not only with each other, but with people of faith the world over; male and female, rich and poor, powerful and weak, experienced and naïve, old and young, global and local, every race and every creed ... all approach the table as equals. As Jesus lay down his authority at the table, so we lay down any remnants of pride, prejudice and self-importance and any feelings of inadequacy, insecurity and hurt. This is a global table, all are welcome, all are equal.

Timeless

Not only is this table one among many across the planet, it is a timeless place ... we eat together in a meal shared by seekers and believers through the ages; Disciples and Desert Fathers, Celts and Catholics, Western puritans and Eastern orthodox, Conservatives and Charismatics, Liberal and Liberationist, the certain and the uncertain, modern and postmodern, the hurting and the healers. In eating together we join in the history of God's church.

Sharing

On that night before he died,
seated in the midst of his community,
your Son, Jesus Christ, took bread;
when he had given you thanks, broke it,
gave it to his disciples, and said:
Take, eat, this is my body which is given for you;
do this to remember me.

After supper he took the cup;
when he had given you thanks,
he gave it to them and said:
This cup is the new covenant
in my blood poured out for you;
do this as often as you drink it to remember me.

And so in this great moment when heaven and earth are manifestly one, we celebrate the mystery of our faith.

Christ has died,
Christ is risen,
Christ will come in glory.

Whether you deserve it or not
Whether you think you deserve it or not
All are welcome
You are welcome
Christ welcomed his brothers and sisters to the table,
he washed them as a servant washes important visitors,
he fed them as parents feed their children,
he laughed with them as friends laugh together,
he blessed them as a host blesses guests,
he loved them as God loves all creation.
Welcome.

Therefore, loving God,
Send your Holy Spirit upon us
that we may be fed
with the body and blood of your Son
and be filled with your life and goodness.
Strengthen us to do your work,
and to be your body in the world.
We are one body because we share in one bread.

Sharing of the bread and wine

Unite us in Christ and give us your peace.
Through your Holy Spirit,
burning as a flame, gentle as a dove,
may we who receive these gifts
live lives of justice, love and prayer,
and be a voice for those who are not heard.

Sir Francis Drake's prayer

Disturb us, Lord, when
We are too well pleased with ourselves,
When our dreams have come true
Because we have dreamed too little,
When we arrived safely
Because we sailed too close to the shore.
Disturb us, Lord, when
With the abundance of things we possess
We have lost our thirst
For the waters of life;
Having fallen in love with life,
We have ceased to dream of eternity
And in our efforts to build a new earth,
We have allowed our vision
Of the new Heaven to dim.
Disturb us, Lord, to dare more boldly,
To venture on wider seas

Where storms will show your mastery;
Where losing sight of land,
We shall find the stars.
We ask You to push back
The horizons of our hopes;
And to push into the future
In strength, courage, hope, and love.

Collect

O God, you manifest in your servants the signs of your presence: Send forth upon us the Spirit of love, that in companionship with one another your abounding grace may increase among us; through Jesus Christ our Lord. **Amen.**

PART 3

Focused on Mission

7

Catching up with God

The church community, participating in God's life, is God's special people, a people living God's life in a covenant of relation and love, a people convinced of its fundamental equality through its common baptism in the name of the triune God. But as communion-in-mission, this image takes on a dynamic meaning as God's people on pilgrimage. God's people chosen not for themselves but for God's purposes.[1]

The way of the pilgrim

What does it mean to be pilgrims today? St Columba, Irish abbot, founder of Iona Abbey and missionary credited with spreading Christianity in present-day Scotland, wrote,

> God counselled Abraham to leave his own country and go in pilgrimage into the land, which God has shown him, to wit the 'Land of Promise'... Now the good counsel which God enjoined here on the father of the faithful is incumbent on all the faithful; that is to leave their country and their land, their wealth and their worldly delight for the sake of the Lord of Elements, and go in perfect pilgrimage in imitation of him.[2]

What a wonderful, if somewhat frightening call, to 'leave one's wealth and worldly delight for the sake of the Lord of Elements'. The Old Testament scholar Walter Brueggemann in *Living Toward a Vision*[3] draws our attention to the status quo of what he calls

---

1 Stephen Bevans and Roger Schroeder, 2004, *Constants in Context: A Theology of Mission for Today*, Maryknoll, NY: Orbis Books, p. 299.

2 Nora Chadwick, 1961, *The Age of the Saints in the Early Celtic Church*, Oxford University Press, p. 82.

3 Walter Brueggemann, 1982, *Living Toward a Vision*, New York: United Church Press

the Brickyard. He tells the story of Moses and Pharaoh and the pivotal moment when Moses refuses to accept that status quo and cries out, 'Let my people go!' At that moment the story can never go back, the relationships have changed, the power has changed, the cat is out of the bag! The same is true for Abraham, once the decision is made to turn his back on Ur things can never be the same again; a whole new story is set in motion, one which still resonates today. And the same is true for God. Once God stepped into the world, reality was fundamentally changed. Eugene Peterson, in his idiomatic translation, *The Message*,[4] rephrases John 1.14 as 'The Word became flesh and blood, and moved into the neighborhood.' This is the reality in which we live and to which we look, a reality where mission is dynamic, where movement is explicit and where it is 'incumbent on all the faithful' to participate with the 'Lord of Elements'.

For many new monastic communities pilgrimage does not simply mean going to a place where we believe God is present; a shrine or holy place. It means fostering a sensitivity and awareness of the presence of God in all the world. This may not be a comfortable experience, it may be hard to encounter God in pain and struggle but as the Brazilian author and poet Paulo Coehlo wrote in *The Pilgrimage*, quoting Rear Admiral Grace Murray Hopper, 'A ship is safest in port, but that's not what ships were made for.' Often now we find the word 'pilgrim' being replaced by 'peregrinate', defined by the Oxford Dictionary as one who 'wanders around from place to place', in the context of faith, holy wanderers. Perhaps the most famous historic peregrinate is the Irish abbot St Brendan. Brendan established several monastic communities but it is for his journey that he is most known and for which he has attracted the epithet the 'navigator'. The great saga, the *Navigatio Sancti Brendani*[5] tells of his seven-year journey from the Dingle peninsula in south west Ireland to what is thought to be America. The story tells how Brendan climbed the mountain near his family home in Dingle to seek God's call. After

4 Eugene Peterson, 2006, *The Message: New Testament, Psalms and Proverbs*, Colorado Springs: Navpress.

5 *Navigatio Sancti Brendani*, http://markjberry.blogs.com/StBrendan.pdf.

spending time looking over the sea from the top of what is now known as Mt Brandon, he built a small leather fishing boat and set sail onto the unknown ocean. As they sailed he encouraged his brothers, saying,

> Fear not, brothers, for our God will be unto us a helper, a mariner, and a pilot; take in the oars and helm, keep the sails set, and may God do unto us, His servants and His little vessel, as He willeth.

A prayer attributed to Francis Drake[6] captures this sense of the dangerous, but rich, way of the peregrinate:

> Disturb us, Lord, when we are too well pleased with ourselves,
> When our dreams have come true
> Because we have dreamed too little,
> When we arrived safely
> Because we sailed too close to the shore.
>
> Disturb us, Lord, to dare more boldly,
> To venture on wider seas
> Where storms will show your mastery;
> Where losing sight of land,
> We shall find the stars.
> We ask you to push back
> The horizons of our hopes;
> And to push into the future
> In strength, courage, hope, and love.

If mission is a pilgrimage into the world then it is by its very nature contextual. What does this mean? It is simply a way of saying that mission never takes place in a vacuum, it always happens with people and in culture. Helmut Thielike, a German theologian of the 1950s, said: 'The gospel must be constantly forwarded to a new address because its recipient is repeatedly changing

---

6 http://markjberry.blogs.com/way_out_west/2006/02/dream_meditatio.html.

his place of residence.'[7] Many new monastic communities were birthed out of this understanding of contextual mission. Mission which means first moving or at least moving one's attention to the heart of the culture. Many are very committed to be present in the places participants of the community live. Some have deliberately moved to places abandoned by the Church or wider society such as inner-city estates which are tough to live in, with a vision of serving God and bringing God's love to places where there is great social deprivation, poverty and community breakdown. Some communities focus more on those who are unwell, addicted or face spiritual impoverishment, who desperately seek meaning, belonging and healing. In all there is the vision of the now, but not yet, kingdom of God, where mission is about catching up with what God is doing.

Contextual mission begins with listening, listening to culture and listening to God. In Chapter 5 we looked at some of the spiritual practices that new monastic communities use to engage with God, but how do we begin to listen to culture? Robert L. Kinast, who has written extensively on theological reflection, says, 'Listening to the culture is the ideal starting point … It avoids the condescending imposition of "what is best" from the outside and it maintains a proper openness and sensitivity to the local culture.'[8]

There are a number of typical ways of listening to culture, functionalist (determining how the parts fit together to form the whole), ecological (determining how the society relates to its physical environment), materialist (determining how the physical environment affects the culture's world view, needs and response to social change) and structuralist (determining the unconscious patterns that shape the culture). All of these are helpful as they begin to paint a big picture of the culture. We also use a semiotic approach which means examining the signs, messages and codes

7 *In Mission Shaped Youth: Rethinking Young People and the Church*, 2007, ed. Tim Sudworth, Graham Cray and Chris Russell, London: Church House Publishing, p. 11.

8 Robert Kinast, 2000, *What are They Saying about Theological Reflection*, Mahwah, NJ: Paulist Press.

that express meaning in that culture. Because of the diversity within any culture, a semiotic approach relies on descriptions from different perspectives, among them inside–outside and speaker–hearer points of view. Another way of putting this is listening to what people say about themselves, their lives and their communities. We listen not only to facts and figures but also to the myths and legends which abound in any culture. These approaches used together can tell us more about communities and the people who inhabit them than the statistics which are far easier to find. Listening to culture is not simply about developing strategies for engaging with it, as Paul says in 1 Thessalonians 2.8, 'Because we loved you so much, we were delighted to share with you not only the gospel of God but our lives as well.'

Listening is an act of love. In sharing life with people, learning about their lives, we also encounter God in new ways:

> Ideally local theology begins with a careful listening to the culture in order to discover the Christ who is already active there. For example, the experience of a hyphenated and marginalized existence felt by so many Hispanic/Latino, African/American and Asian American communities has led to a deeper identification with Jesus as a 'marginalised Jew.'[9]

This can be a very ordinary thing. At 3 a.m. on New Year's Day 2009, Mark was serving at safespace's Sank•tuary project (see below) when a lady came in to the night cafe. She had taken off her shoe as she left a night club and had unfortunately stood on a broken bottle. As Mark knelt and removed bits of glass from her foot and cleaned it of blood and dirt, he felt a sudden and tangible connection to the moment Jesus washed the feet of the disciples. In that moment the story in John 13 became very real and took on new meaning, not only for Mark but for the whole community of safespace.

This practice of holding together culture and gospel is known as 'contextual theology'. In his book, *Models of Contextual*

---

9 Ibid.

Theology, Stephen Bevans[10] identifies six models of contextual theology practice. New monastic communities tend to focus on two of these models in practice. The first is what Bevans calls the 'Transcendental' model. This is based on an understanding that there is common human experience of God which may get lost in the complexity of life and of bad experiences of religion. Moot, for example, runs two groups during the week, the first called 'Serum' presupposes that God is involved in people's lives, but because of lack of experience or of language they are not always aware or able to recognize and engage with God. This carries some sense of Paul's address to the people of Athens on the Mars Hill.

> Paul then stood up in the meeting of the Areopagus and said: 'People of Athens! I see that in every way you are very religious. For as I walked around and looked carefully at your objects of worship, I even found an altar with this inscription: to an unknown god. So you are ignorant of the very thing you worship – and this is what I am going to proclaim to you. The God who made the world and everything in it is the Lord of heaven and earth and does not live in temples built by human hands. And he is not served by human hands, as if he needed anything. Rather, he himself gives everyone life and breath and everything else. From one man he made all the nations, that they should inhabit the whole earth; and he marked out their appointed times in history and the boundaries of their lands. God did this so that they would seek him and perhaps reach out for him and find him, though he is not far from any one of us. "For in him we live and move and have our being."' (Acts 17.22–28)

The second activity is 'Stressed in the City', an open event for workers in the City of London. Here the community uses stillness and the meditations of John Main, a Roman Catholic Bene-dictine monk and priest who, when living at Ealing Abbey in west London, developed a meditation technique based on those of the

10 Stephen Bevans, 2008, *Models of Contextual Theology* (Faith and Cultures Series), Maryknoll, NY: Orbis Books, p. 37ff.

desert fathers which uses a prayer-phrase or mantra. Use of these techniques, the creative arts and story are intended to help people move beyond negative experiences and feelings about religion and to find new meaning. For new monastic communities this isn't only about what they do or offer, but about how they engage at a personal and community level with the people and communities they live among. The desire to live lives which challenge the negative perceptions and experiences of Christianity in our culture is a common aim; to visibly model a way of being Christian which encourages others to think again about God.

As well as this Transcendental model many new monastic communities are exploring forms of theological reflection and practice which bring experience and the gospel together in a continuous spiral of practice and reflection so that daily living is transformed and meaning is made for the whole community. Bevans calls this the 'Praxis' model of contextual theology. The story of safespace's Sank•tuary project is an example of this.

In November 2008 safespace was gathered together for their regular Thursday meal, spending time reflecting on the encounter between Jesus and the Samaritan woman at the well related in John 4. In the silence they focused on how Jesus broke social taboos, community boundaries, gender politics, social norms and religious rules for the sake of this messed-up individual. The question arose, *What would it look like for us here in Telford?* One of the community spoke about the hundreds of young people on the streets in the early hours of Sunday morning, young people who week in and week out get themselves into a mess, a mess of their own making but a mess nonetheless. Within three weeks Sank•tuary, a free night cafe/safe haven, had opened and was working on the streets outside the local night club. Within four months the police reported that crime in that location had fallen 30 per cent. During the time that Sank•tuary has been serving Telford a number of non-church young people have volunteered for the project; this, unlike other night club ministries, is part of the purpose of Sank•tuary. Working together is a way for community members and others to reflect together about how serving changes our thinking, our living and our understanding of God.

What is central to both of these models is presence. New monastic communities are on the whole communities who actively live their daily lives in the context of culture and see mission as a direct and unavoidable consequence of this.

Lesslie Newbigin, British theologian, missiologist, missionary and author wrote:

> We have good news to tell ... It is not communicated if the question uppermost in our minds is about the survival of the church in the inner city. Because our society is a pagan society, and because Christians have in general failed to realize how radical is the contradiction between the Christian vision and the assumptions that we breathe in from every part of our shared existence, we allow ourselves to be deceived into thinking of the church as one of the many 'good causes' which need our support and which will collapse if they are not adequately supported. If our 'evangelism' is at bottom an effort to shore up the tottering fabric of the church (and it sometimes looks like that) then it will not be heard as good news. The church is in God's keeping. We do not have the right to be anxious about it. We have our Lord's word that the gates of hell shall not prevail against it. The nub of the matter is that we have been chosen to be the bearers of good news for the whole world, and the question is simply whether we are faithful in communicating it.[11]

The way of God

> With what shall I come before the Lord and bow down before the exalted God? Shall I come before him with burnt offerings, with calves a year old? Will the Lord be pleased with thousands of rams, with ten thousand rivers of olive oil? Shall I offer my firstborn for my transgression, the fruit of my body for the sin of my soul? He has shown you, O mortal, what is good. And

---

11 Lesslie Newbigin, 1994, *A Word in Season: Perspectives on Christian World Missions*, Grand Rapids, MI: Eerdmans, p. 41.

what does the Lord require of you? To act justly and to love mercy and to walk humbly with your God. (Micah 6.6–8)

There is a wonderful simplicity in the prophet Micah's words; in a real way he encapsulates the new monastic calling. In it is blown away all notion of religion as observance, duty or identity and focuses the mind on a missional dynamic.

1. *To act justly* Being honest and fair in the way communities live our lives. In today's world this is highly significant and very practical! It challenges individuals and communities about the ethics of living in the world. If new monastic communities desire to live an exposed life then justice is not just about buying a few fair trade items but doing all our business in a way which is and is seen to be rigorously fair and just. It means allowing others to truly be themselves and taking their concerns and struggles seriously, making time for others beyond our own selfish concerns; it means stepping back and allowing others to lead when we know they have the gifts, not being in love with power and creating space for others to contribute equally even if we think we can do it better! Acting in a way which intends to transform injustice in society, standing firm against inequality and abuse – locally and globally. Yes, this has a political aspect but it also has a relational aspect. It does mean big things, campaigns and charity work, but it also means how we change society by our local actions and involvement, how we act and live as peacemakers where we are. Giving others what they deserve, what they are worth! There is no sliding scale or metre for this. It must be simple, we treat others as they were made, as creations of God, as made in the image of God. So, as hard as it may seem we have to begin by looking through what life has made them to see the reflection of the divine which may be deep, deep within. That is not to excuse or condone behaviour but to try to love them as God made them and to demand from others that everyone is treated with the same justice, the same starting point, the same rights, the same respect and the same freedoms.

2. *To love mercy* While we demand justice for all and live justly we are called at all times to act with mercy. Not to seek equality or rights for ourselves but to live servant lives, in the way of the Christ – the servant king – and to relish, to love doing it! It also means that our way needs to be God's way of compassion. This is not about our rights, or our sense of being treated badly. Today, when we might perceive ourselves as being the persecuted minority, we ought to stop, step back and look first at what others experience. If we want to gain respect we must do it not by complaining and fighting but by being the defenders of others despite the way we ourselves are treated. Justice and mercy go hand-in-hand; we demand justice for others and put aside our own demands for justice, instead acting with total mercy. We fight for the rights of others and lay down our own rights.

3. *Walk humbly with your God* God is an intimate and immanent God, a God who does not want to dictate to us from 'on high' but to journey with us on a daily basis. Walking with God in God's world is not a discipline but a privilege. We are always learning, always discovering more about God and the possibility of God. That relationship is not a located one but a lived one. In Chapter 4 we talked about exploring/discovering how we develop a 'rhythm' of spirituality that is woven through daily life and living rather than it being focused on one moment each week. Hospitality is a common theme within the missiology and thinking of new monastic communities but here the challenge is not how communities welcome the stranger, but how we are good guests as well as good hosts. Luke chapter 10 has Jesus, in an echo of Jeremiah 29, instructing the 72 to eat what is put before them and to become part of the family business, the economic unit.

In the words of God through Micah, we receive a picture of restored relationship, a foretaste of the mission of Jesus, even the mission of the Trinity – God's mission, fulfilled in Jesus, accomplished through the Spirit and in which we participate. This mission is a mission of reconciliation and restored relationships.

This is the heart of the prayer that Jesus prays in John 17.20–23:

> My prayer is not for them alone. I pray also for those who will believe in me through their message, that all of them may be one, Father, just as you are in me and I am in you. May they also be in us so that the world may believe that you have sent me. I have given them the glory that you gave me, that they may be one as we are one – I in them and you in me – so that they may be brought to complete unity. Then the world will know that you sent me and have loved them even as you have loved me.

For new monastic communities mission and evangelism is about transformation and growing – human becoming – in a culture that is losing a sense of what it means to be human, let alone what it is to be Christian. Mission and spiritual fulfilment have traditionally been seen as the fulfilment of going to heaven once you have died. New monastics are committed to a more transformative sense of salvation; the life and work of the Trinity in the present as well as the future. The good news of the kingdom is the transformation of individuals, communities and culture; the coming of shalom. Stanley Grenz says:

> Living as a community carries with it a prophetic dimension. Insofar as we model community, our presence bears prophetic witness to the world. It issues an implicit call to society to measure itself against the divine reign under which it too must stand and against which it will be judged. This presence is itself a prophetic evangelization of the world. For it carries the implicit call to the world to acknowledge the Lordship of the God who has established us as his people.[12]

The mission to which the Church is invited to participate is prophetic, it is also dynamic, as Howard Snyder, a professor at Tyndale Seminary in Canada writes:

---

12 Stanley Grenz, 1994, *Theology for the Community of God*, Nashville: Broadman & Holman, p. 503.

Mission in Trinitarian perspective is never one-way. We do not simply go out in mission because the Trinity send us. Rather, mission is reciprocal. In response to God's grace we carry out our mission to God and thus are 'carried' into mission in the world by the Holy Spirit, who in fact goes ahead of us ... The church is essentially a community in mission and in movement. This is so because of who God is as Trinity and how he is manifesting himself in the world.[13]

The Orthodox tradition suggests that this dynamic begins with liturgy, the Eucharist, the moment in which we share in bread (one body) and blood, the new covenant of love for all creation. Liturgy is defined as 'the work of the people', meaning the ways in which we engage and re-engage with the community of God. Mission thus is the 'liturgy after the liturgy', the 'work of the people' after 'the work of the people'. Romanian Orthodox theologian Father Ion Bria[14] described 'the liturgy after the liturgy' as having four aspects:

1. An ongoing reaffirming of the true Christian identity, fullness and integrity, which have to be constantly renewed by the Eucharistic communion.
2. To enlarge the space for witness by creating a new Christian milieu, each in his own environment: family, society, office, factory, etc., is not a simple matter of converting the non-Christians in the vicinity of the parishes, but also a concern for finding room where the Christians live and work and where they can publicly exercise their witness and worship.
3. The liturgical life has to nourish the Christian life not only in its private sphere, but also in its public and political realm. Therefore, the installation in history of a visible Christian fellowship, which overcomes human barriers against justice, freedom and unity, is a part of that liturgy after the liturgy.

13 Howard Snyder and Daniel Runyon, 2002, *Decoding the Church*, Grand Rapids, MI: Baker Books, p. 55.
14 http://www.rondtb.msk.ru/info/en/Bria_en.htm (accessed 2013).

4. Liturgy means public and collective action and therefore there is a sense in which the Christian is a creator of community; this particular charisma has crucial importance today with the increasing lack of human fellowship in society. The Christian has to be a continual builder of a true koinonia of love and peace even if he is politically marginal and lives in a hostile surrounding.

safespace say of their experience of the liturgy of the Eucharist:

For a while we've been talking about the two-fold vitality of the communion meal for us (when we use the word vital, we mean both senses i.e. essential and life-giving) – vital in drawing and binding us a communion/community before and with God/each other (a process in which we are adopted into a God who is community) and vital in drawing and binding us into mission (a process in which we are adopted into a God who is incarnate and dynamic), we talk about the communion as the life-blood of mission. This is something that has arisen from our experience as a community rather than some applied God-knowledge. It is not a strategy we have adopted but a reality we have experienced.

These experiences have moved us to fall in love with the Trinity in a new way, a way which now shapes our glimpses of God and our instinct for Church, the mutuality and the mystery, the love and the living, the forgiveness and the fruitfulness, the compassion and the connections. The communion draws our eye to God incarnate and sacramental, to a sent God and a sacrificial God (was it any harder for the Son to be separated from the Parent than it was for the Parent to be separated from the Son?). A God who creates in community, who redeems in community and who sustains in community – source, word and breath. It is no surprise then that we find ourselves deepest in God when we are in community, when we find ourselves loving others, forgiving others, seeing God in others, giving ourselves in surrender to others and significantly breaking bread with others. We are one body because we all share in one bread.

A Liturgy from safespace

God calls us into the divine presence,
we come because we are called,
we come because we are called in,
we come because we are called out.

The liturgy after the liturgy.
There is no breathing out without breathing in,
There is no flow without ebb,
There is no outpouring without drinking deep of life.

We cannot be love for the community without being drawn
deeper ourselves into God. We cannot bring change to the
world without our lives being realigned. We cannot forgive
each other without knowing the freedom of forgiveness ourselves. We ache for the loneliness of the world and are known
by a God who is family. We cry for a world trapped in greed
and are loved by a God who gave up everything. We fight
against a world with little justice and are embraced by a God
of mercy.

Forgive us Lord for not taking the time to know you more,
Forgive us Lord for not taking the time to know each other
    more,
Forgive us Lord for not taking the time to know your world
    more.

You welcome us back with simple open arms,
forgiven, restored, ready to begin work again,
You stand naked, mocked and bleeding
with the love of a proud parent on your face,
You move in and amongst us with un-ignorable force, yet
    tenderly,

This moment is not the end of the road,
It is the beginning of a new stage of the journey,

For God so loved the world – may we naturally follow suit,
That he gave his only Son – may we learn the wonder of
  sacrifice,
That all who believe – may our love for one another be the
  crucial evidence,
May not perish – may we work to halt the collapse of lives,
  of communities and of creation,
But have eternal life – may we point to the hope you bring
  now and for the future.
It is time to walk on,
this time we walk together,
with each other and with God.

It is time to walk on for God's purpose and God's people,
giving our lives as a living sacrifice, we walk together, with
  each other and with God.
For we are one body because we share in one bread,
And one in the spirit because we drink from one cup.[15]

New monastic communities on the whole have been birthed from
a spirit of creativity; a need to find a way of community living;
worship and mission which grow from the real and raw experience of community members and the culture in which they dwell.
Liturgy then emerges from this desire to connect in deeper ways
with God, each other and the world. It grows from the bottom
up, and while rooted in the history and experience of the Church
through the ages it also reflects communities' ongoing life in the
world.

God's intent to establish community with creation is a central
theme of the entire biblical message ... Taken as a whole the
Bible asserts that God directs his program to the bringing about
of community in the highest sense of the word – a redeemed
people, living within a renewed creation, and enjoying the
presence of their God.[16]

15 Text and liturgy from safespace.
16 Grenz, *Theology for the Community of God*, p. 112ff.

8

Getting beyond Them and Us

Justice is achieved not in striving for justice but with love.

Tolstoy

There is only one law of life which is really precious: though you meet with injustice at every turn, remain humble.

Marcus Aurelius

Surrendering power and the way of Christian discipleship

For centuries the Church has been caught up in dualistic thinking that has prevented people from coming to a full understanding of the purposes of the mission of Jesus Christ. We have tended to define ourselves in opposition to certain groups – we are Catholics because we don't like Evangelicals, or we are Traditionalists when we don't like Progressives. The truth is that we as the Church have played this game both with theology and with our under-standing of church for centuries, and this has impoverished our ability to truly love as well as be effective in following God into the world for the purposes of mission and evangelism.

It is our belief that new monastics seek to challenge this either-or approach to life as being excluding and violent, and instead seek to follow in the way of Jesus, to be 'both-and'. This then puts the emphasis on unity in diversity, learning to live in unity when we may not agree, which is the implication of living the new commandment as the highpoint of the gospel for monastics. So this both-and approach recognizes that we are catholic and evangelical, traditional and radical, theologically rooted in think-ing and practical in outreach. This comes from a commitment to hold both incarnational and redemptive theology in tension. This is not easy, but surely this is what Christ's commandment to love God, love ourselves and love others is all about – getting beyond the binary mode of dualistic thinking because few things are ever black and white – life is more complicated than that.

When Jesus healed people and worked on the Sabbath, when he spoke and touched unclean people, when he prevented men from stoning a woman to death, he was demonstrating that Christian discipleship is about living and acting in non-dualistic ways – an obedience to follow God, who in weakness, death and resurrection seeks to restore all things back into restored relationship with the divine.

To live this way, new monastic communities seek to be virtuous (that is, not being fearful, greedy, angry or resentful but instead peaceable, generous, loving and gracious) as well as committing to spiritual practices that enable us to live this Christian discipleship of non-dualistic thinking and acting through the love of God.

So new monasticism is a distinctive model of church as this focus on non-dualistic thinking and acting promotes a healthy and mature approach to the Christian faith.

If there is one thing that excites us about new monasticism, it is the many differing forms of it now blossoming all over the post-industrial Western world in all denominations and traditions. (If you doubt this, there is even a Southern Baptist expression of new monasticism in French-speaking Quebec in Canada!) It is a joy that these cover the full range of church denominations and traditions, unsettling institutions to recover a sense of generous community. There is a recovery of unity in diversity: Protestants are working with Catholics, low-church sensibilities with high ones, and sacramental with charismatic. In a Church that in modernity has been characterized by conflict and power games, there is a strong commitment by many today to identify with being Christian beyond denominational and traditional allegiances, and the need to get beyond the binary wars of a Church in blatant disunity. The collaboration of Christians working together in difference and in love, celebrating what they have in common, in humility, is a truly wonderful thing.

Our excitement and hope for new monasticism is that as a dynamic expression of church, it can redress the problems created with church in 'Christendom' mode, that is, one defined by power, privilege and wealth over people. Now, in our post-Christendom, postmodern and post-secular context, we are excited that the Church is rediscovering its call to a ministry of love, powerlessness, vulnerability and service. New monasticism is an expression of this. From its birth, monasticism was a reaction against the abuses of the Church as Christendom, chiefly when it became the state religion of the Roman Empire. Christians deliberately went into the Syrian and Egyptian deserts to escape the oppression of church as 'dominant political society'.

New monastics, again following the tradition of the desert mothers and fathers, are rediscovering the politics of powerlessness and giving power away. As Shane Claiborne, founder of the Simple Way and the Potter Street community in Philadelphia, said:

> Many beautiful Christians working for social change in a range of movements believe we can bring about fundamental change by using power benevolently rather than reworking the power equation. We see ourselves as the good guys who will use our influence for justice – and perhaps, in these terms, we succeed in getting our candidate on the ballot or elected. But the Christ we follow has a different, harder path – one of downward mobility, of struggling to become the least, of joining those at the bottom.[1]

Inspired by the Franciscans, new monastics seek to follow the example set by Jesus in the Beatitudes as a particular missional imperative. Now that the Church is increasingly losing power, this focus on servant discipleship is a deliberate approach inspired by Christ the servant and loving teacher. So we follow Jesus Christ as our example, Saviour and Lord (Philippians 3.10).

We hope new monastic communities will be resilient in following this approach to powerlessness to resist and challenge the

---

1 http://www.onbeing.org/program/Monastic-revolution/feature/downward-mobility-upscale-world/526 (accessed 1/8/13).

new Christendom, which is the rise of fundamentalist expressions of the Christian Church that are keen to define who is and who is not acceptable to belong to the Church. In some countries, churches are colluding with national governments in outlawing and oppressing minority groups in society to keep transgressors and sinners far away from church and society, focused on a punitive system of purity. This is the very issue that Jesus shouts at the Pharisees and Sadducees about in the Gospel stories, because such an approach is contrary to the mission of love and reconciliation of God: You who are without sin can cast the first stone. This is an aggressive power discourse which we hope new monasticism will stand up to, by living a call to unconditional loving service and humility to a world and a Church in need, inspired by God the Creator, Redeemer and Spirit.

For the last 200 years, some elements of the Church have focused on an identity predicated on not liking particular groups of people. These have been slaves, disabled people, women, ethnic minorities, divorced people and, most recently, gay people. This is a sign of an expression of church seeking to have power over people, a Church in Christendom mode, a Church wanting to define who is in and who is out. New monasticism has stood up to this, focusing on Christ's call to love and bring justice and not judgement. Now, more than ever, we need new monastic voices to challenge the increasingly hardline fundamentalist calls, emphasizing love and justice with humility.

The vision of Larson and Osborne writing in 1970 about their hopes for the emerging church was for a Church that was contextual and experimental in mission, for new forms of church, for the removal of barriers and division, for a blend of evangelism and social action, for attention to both experience and tradition and the breakdown of clergy/laity distinctions. At the time this was inspiring, but the vision still rings true with new monastic communities as expressions of emerging and fresh expressions of church, called to:

• Rediscover contextual and experimental mission in the western church.

- Forms of church that are not restrained by institutional expectations.
- Be open to change and God wanting to do a new thing.
- Use the word ... 'and'. Whereas the heady polarities of our day seek to divide us into an either-or camp, the mark of the emerging church will be its emphasis on both-and. For generations we have divided ourselves into camps: Protestants and Catholics, high church and low, clergy and laity, social activists and personal piety, liberals and conservatives, sacred and secular, instructional and underground.
- Bring together the most helpful of the old and the best of the new, blending the dynamic of a personal gospel with the compassion of social concern.
- Find its ministry being expressed by a whole people, wherein the distinction between clergy and laity will be that of function, not of status or hierarchical division.
- In the emerging Church, due emphasis will be placed on both theological rootage and contemporary experience, on celebration in worship and involvement in social concerns, on faith and feeling, reason and prayer, conversion and continuity, the personal and the conceptual.[2]

To do this, we need to be committed to an identity of seeking to be Christian as a prerogative for the third millennium, which, as Larson and Osborne have said, has to be about getting beyond the wars of church traditions which are about power discourse and fear of the other. To do this, we have to recover a broad and generous understanding of what 'being Christian is all about'.

New monasticism, if we choose it, could be a corrective to the abuses of the past, as there remains the very real danger that we will still continue to define ourselves by tribal labels: Evangelical, Catholic, Liberal, Episcopal, Lutheran, Roman, Liberationist, Emergent and so on – before we use the word Christian. In so doing we continue the ongoing disunity of the Church, where we impoverish ourselves by not having a higher regard to Christ's

2 B. Larson, R. Osborne, 1970, *The Emerging Church*, London: Word Books, pp. 9–11.

new commandment: By this may all people know that you are my disciples, if you have love one for another.

Our hope for the Church and for new monasticism as an expression of ecclesial community is that we start with being Christian and with the call to imitate Christ as a renewed passion, rather than with tribal labels that emphasize difference. This will enable the Church of today to maintain a calling to love, over and above the corrosive and divisive focus of the Church in modernity as focused on judgementalism, difference (on the excuse of purity) and arrogance.

One corrective that new monasticism makes is that it draws on both incarnational and redemptive theologies. For centuries, the Church has been divided by these two overarching theologies that both bring an important contribution to the Christian faith. The Church has quite literally been divided by an unholy binary of an either-or understanding of these theologies, and not sustained by a healthy and deeply Christian both-and. If one can imagine Christian theology as a continuum, then all the theologies in the world break down roughly into these two great visions, one incarnational and one redemptive. This is represented by the see-saw diagram below. Throughout the Church's history these traditions have been locked into a terrible battle about which is the more important. So throughout history the see-saw has swung, at times with redemptive theology being in the dominant position, and at other times, incarnational theology being the major influence.[3]

INCARNATIONAL THEOLOGY	REDEMPTIVE THEOLOGY

INCARNATIONAL THEOLOGY	REDEMPTIVE THEOLOGY
• Jesus as fully human	• Jesus as fully God
• Grace and Love	• Sin and Repentance
• High regard to justice, culture, being human and social action	• High regard to mission and evangelism

3 Inspired by the work of Stephen Bevans, 2002, *Models of Contextual Theology* (Faith and Cultures Series), New York: Orbis Books, pp. 1–2, 5, 7.

Both theologies stem from Christians having wrestled with the nature and importance of Jesus, who is both fully God and fully human. Traditionally, the Church has struggled with the complexity of holding these two truths concerning the nature of Jesus in tension, and different theological perspectives have tended to either focus on Jesus' humanity or on his divinity. Where you start with these two theologies holds implications for how you see people and the world.

If you are fond of redemptive theology, then your belief could well begin with the story of original sin, and that the whole cosmos is broken; that God now seeks to restore all things by people facing up to their sin, repenting, and living a just life worthy of being a follower of God. The world continues to be lost, and ruined by evil, and that world now waits for the day of judgement when God as Christ will judge all before the beginning of a renewed earth and renewed heaven in a restored cosmos. Justice and mercy are important here, but not as important as repentance and the call for holiness. Easter and the resurrection are in this view the great celebration in the Church's liturgical year. Churches that are very redemptive in their theology tend to focus on the letters of Paul in the New Testament, as well as Old Testament texts which talk of the need for repentance and God's judgement of humanity.

If you are an adherent of incarnational theology, then your belief begins with the gift of Jesus who comes as a human as a sign of God's love to the world. Jesus expresses God's mission of love and mercy, to restore all things back into right relationship through the loving mystery of God's mission of reconciliation. For those who start with this theology, Christmas is the high point of the year, as the gift of God's grace coming in love and powerlessness to befriend and heal humanity. The texts that are most often referred to in this tradition, are the stories of Christ's life in the Gospels, and particularly the Gospel of John. Jesus, then, is about building an expression of a just community, as the new kingdom of God, one focused on justice and love, and inclusive of all those who are excluded in our world. Concerning the cross, Jesus comes not in weakness but as a strong person who dies quickly and with dignity on the cross. Jesus' death is not to appease an angry God,

but to break down all the political and spiritual divisions that prevent the kingdom of God being realized on earth. In effect, Jesus
is dying for our anger, and not God's.

Admittedly, we have characterized these two positions very
broadly, but these have largely been the position of the two theologies in modernity. The truth is that we need both. What excites
us about new monasticism, emerging and fresh expressions of
church, is that there appears to be a renewed importance to a
both-and position. For example you will hear Shane Claiborne as
an evangelical new monastic be passionate about justice and the
need to serve the poor, challenging evangelicals who are largely
redemptive in disposition, to face the importance of incarnational
theology. We have also heard new monastics coming from a more
liberal and catholic sensibility who are challenging their church
traditions to have a higher view of redemptive theology and the
importance of holiness and personal piety.

As a whole, new monastics are able to hold on to these two
positions, and they embrace a healthy theology as well as healthy
expressions of Church for today because they are committed to
non-dualistic and non-dichotomizing thinking and acting. We are
learning in mission that people need to experience the love of God
– the truth of incarnational theology as a starting position – to
then realize that they and we are broken, and that all of us need
healing and to focus on repentance and right living as we grow
in our humanity and faith – and that means growing into the
importance of redemptive theology.

So we come back to the heart of the matter, that in new monasticism we encounter a call to love God, love ourselves and love
others as the focus of Christian discipleship, being led by the
Spirit of life. This is both an individual journey of letting go of
the need to achieve and the desire for riches and power, and striving instead for a willingness to live closely with others, which
again comes at some personal cost. This is a disposition to being
open to God, which requires people to let go of the so-called
'prosperity gospel' (a Christian religious doctrine that financial
blessing is the will of God for Christians, and that faith, positive
speech, and donations to Christian ministries will always increase

one's material wealth), individualistic consumptive gratification, Anglo-Saxon middle-class aspirations, and a willingness for life to become uncertain, sacrificial and costly. The rewards of inner wholeness and enriched community life are significant, but the call to this way of life is, from the start, costly. So new monasticism needs people to model this way of life to enable others to experience it, lest it seem extreme or frightening, as it requires the individual to face her or his wounded inner self.

Humility, as we explored in the Benedictine tradition, is a quality and calling for Christians in the present age, because it recognizes Christ's call to us, to imitate the character of Jesus as expressed in Paul's letter to the Philippians (2.1–8):

> If then there is any encouragement in Christ, any consolation from love, any sharing in the Spirit, any compassion and sympathy, make my joy complete: be of the same mind, having the same love, being in full accord and of one mind. Do nothing from selfish ambition or conceit, but in humility regard others as better than yourselves. Let each of you look not to your own interests, but to the interests of others. Let the same mind be in you that was in Christ Jesus, who, though he was in the form of God, did not regard equality with God as something to be exploited, but emptied himself, taking the form of a slave, being born in human likeness. And being found in human form, he humbled himself and became obedient to the point of death – even death on a cross.

Humility expresses an important quality of mature Christianity: a calling to a whole-of-life approach to discipleship; a way of life that we hope will assist people to see the authenticity of the Church and encounter the living God.

A story from the Far East

Korea has a very tumultuous recent history. In 1910 the indigenous dynastic monarchies finally fell to the might of the Japanese and Korea became part of that empire. Of course this only lasted until the defeat of Japan in the Second World War, followed by the partition of Korea along the same lines as we experienced in Europe with East and West Germany – with the Soviets in control of the North and the US in the South. In the 1950s the country suffered what has become known as the forgotten war, when the North invaded the South and a very bloody and catastrophic conflict ensued. The Korean War affected everyone, people were displaced, millions killed and the land ravaged. Eventually the Northern Army was pushed back to the 38th parallel and peace was restored, though of course the North and South are technically still in a state of war. Democracy did not follow immediately on from the war for the South, in fact after a coup in 1961 it was under a military government until the 1980s and the ordinary people of South Korea suffered many abuses of their freedom and human rights.

In this context of turmoil a new thinking emerged, which became known as 'Minjung' – meaning 'Mass' or 'the People' – and a student movement began to grow from the 'Han' of the people. Han, as Minjung poet, Chi-Ha Kim wrote is, 'the Minjung's anger and sad sentiment turned inward, hardened and stuck to their hearts. "Han" is caused as one's outgoingness is blocked and pressed for an extended period of time by external oppression and exploitation.'[4] A. Sung Park writes in an article on Minjung and Process Hermeneutics:

> The Minjung are the down-trodden whose unmistakable sign is Han-brooding. Han is the compressed feeling of suffering caused by injustice and oppression, a complex feeling of resentment and helplessness, anger and lamentation. Han is potential energy, an active volcano of indignation and agony. Depending on how it is unraveled, Han may turn out to be creative energy for revolution or may explode destructively to seek revenge and killing. The Minjung Han of women is more intense than any other because of the double bind of women in patriarchal and

---

4 http://www.cms-uk.org/tabid/151/articleType/articleView/4275/Breaking-koreas-vicious-circle.aspx

hierarchical culture. Traditional folk songs and folk tales are full of the Minjung Han of women.[5]

This student movement was led, among others, by many seminary students, priests in training. They believed that the Han of the people should not result in hate and destruction but that a positive transforming 'Dan' needed to be born. Dan has two dimensions; at the personal level, Dan means self-denial; at the social level it means to cut off the vicious circle of Minjung's Han and revenge. The emerging Minjung theologians believed that instead of hate arising from oppression and injustice, rather the experience should birth a new way of life which grew from sharing and love. They believed that you cannot defeat power and abuse with more power and abuse, rather you must kill hate by self-denying love.

For the poet Kim, the dialectic unification of Han and Dan means to undergo the four stages of revolution. The first stage is 'inviting God in the heart' (Shi-Chun-Ju), the second stage is 'letting God grow in the body' (Yan-Chun-Ju), the third stage is 'practising the struggle for embodying God' (Haeng-Chun-Ju), the fourth stage is 'living as humble and resurrected champions of the Minjung beyond death' (Sang-Chun-Ju). For Kim, revolution for social justice and revolution for individual spirituality are one. This dialectic unification of Han and Dan liberates the Minjung from self-destruction by transforming their Han into creative revolution.[6]

It was from this Minjung theology that the Sharing Houses grew. The mission of the Sharing Houses is described by founder Revd Kim, Hong-Il as,

to reach 'new persons' and 'new communities' founded on the gospel through living with the poor ... supporting the poor to help themselves solve their own problems ... supporting them to discover and experiment in ways of living in cooperation,

---

5 http://www.religion-online.org/showarticle.asp?title=2746 (accessed 15/3/13).
6 http://www.biblicalstudies.org.uk/pdf/ijt/33-4_001.pdf (accessed 15/3/13).

solidarity and love in their real life ... restoring the image of God inscribed in the poor people, bridging the gaps between the gospel and the world, beliefs and life and embodying the world of sharing and cooperation ... [they] provide the ground and driving forces for these values to be realised in real life. Activities of the Sharing House are purposed to contribute to the dissemination of [the] gospel to the poor and serve them according to the guide of Jesus Christ who is the foundation of our Church.[7]

There are now around 70 Sharing Houses in South Korea, working with children, abused women, orphans, migrant workers, the homeless, etc. They teach languages and skills, start social enterprises to provide work, provide counselling, shelter and most of all love.

What is being explored in South Korea is a theology and a mission which begins with the heart, the passion (the Han) of the people (the Minjung) but rooting the mission not in reactionary zeal but in an attempt to live God's love (as the Dan) in community. A. Sung Park writes:

Minjung theology is not primarily concerned about the Korean Christians in particular, but the oppressed Korean Minjung in general. This theology specifically discovers the deep-seated feeling of Han in the Minjung and endeavors to transform it through Dan ... to cut off 'the vicious circle' of the Minjung's Han by exorcizing the evil spirit of revenge against the oppressive rulers from the Han-ridden hearts of the Minjung and by transforming the Han into the power of revolution for establishing God's nation.[8]

While the Sharing House communities would not necessarily describe themselves as new monastic communities, much of what can be witnessed in South Korea illustrates well this desire for

---

7 From a document given to the authors by Revd Kim, Hong-Il.
8 http://www.religion-online.org/showarticle.asp?title=2746 (accessed 15/3/13).

community as whole-of-life discipleship at the heart of the culture. The Sharing House movement is a network of communities, all of whom are distinct and unique; they emerge from a life of spirituality, mission as peacemaking and discipleship in a context, and as such are a vibrant example of authentic Christian community and discipleship.

As we reflect on what whole-of-life discipleship looks like for us we remember the Benedictus, or the Song of Zechariah, recited by monastics and friars in morning prayer of the Daily Office for over two millennia.

In the tender compassion of our God
the dawn from on high shall break upon us,
to shine on those who dwell in darkness and the shadow of
  death,
and to guide our feet into the way of peace.
Amen.

This is our prayer for new monasticism, in our increasingly perilous and complex world.

9

Formation and Discipleship

The Sermon on the Mount isn't just an ideal vision for a new society. It is a sustainable way of life for those who live by faith.[1]

The great challenges for Christianity in the third millennium are the tasks of formation and discipleship (or catechesis) with 'never-and-dechurched' people who are not interested in religion but either pursue their own spiritual paths or who have come reluctantly to accept a life of pain or lack of meaning. This is because they are unlikely to commit to Christian training courses such as Alpha, Beta and Emmaus, among others.

Many of these approaches have been aimed at professional workers who are open to argument and exploration in a training course format. Yet this approach is not transferable into every context. As Graham Cray, the Archbishops' Missioner, has said, 'we meet in our weakness, where all the resources of the various church traditions are increasingly ineffective, where people simply don't relate to taught courses, so we have to explore new ways of doing discipleship'.[2] Church organizations in the post-industrial Western world are left with a number of questions about how to do evangelism and discipleship, needing new approaches and resources for such engagement.

Before exploring this further, we must first understand what we mean by 'the faith', 'formation' and 'conversion'. For faith, new monastics have placed an emphasis on orthopraxis (right action/living) rather than orthodoxy (right thinking). In the period from

---

1 Jonathan Wilson-Hartgrove, *New Monasticism: What It Has to Say to Today's Church*, Grand Rapids, MI: Brazos, p. 33.

2 Recorded at the Fresh Expressions Round Table Number 5 Meeting, Lambeth Palace, October 2009.

the Enlightenment to the modern period, faith became a set of propositional facts synthesized out of the ecumenical creeds, which churches required you to be able to affirm and then repent of your former thinking to then become a Christian. Here we would wish to make a critique: that this form of faith is far too 'in your head' and over-focused on conceptual thinking. Conversion must go much deeper than this. In a recent interview for an American radio show, Jean Vanier, founder of the L'Arche community, challenged this over-thinking approach.[3] For him, a more authentic and deeper understanding of conversion was less about thinking and more about a change in attitude and behaviour. Faith and conversion are, therefore, about the orientation of the heart, taking the step to follow the Christian God of love.

Conversion is about the whole of life. It is about changing our attitude not only to knowing God, but how we view our money, how we see marginalized people, how we interact with them, and how we respond to the call to participate in the *ekklesia* (church community) of love and fraternity. Conversion is far more than changing your ideas, it's a lifestyle change. In the interview, Jean Vanier went on to say that the Greek word for faith was the same as trust. This form of faith is not exclusively about belief but, as Vanier said, we need to trust in God, trust in community and trust in people. So when we talk of discipleship, we need to look back into more ancient understandings to reframe our perspectives. Discipleship, then, is a process of ongoing conversion, growing in trust of God, and seeking to live a way that resonates deeply with following Christ.

New monastics have responded in a whole-of-life approach to assist 'conversion' to the Christian faith by inviting people to engage with the community relationally, in helping others, in attending spirituality discussion groups, and through involvement in contemplative prayer and worship and forms of mentoring. These activities aim to enable people to experience and encounter God, to perceive that God is real and relevant in their own understanding and for their own unique spiritual journey. Conversion

---

3 Jean Vanier, The Wisdom of Tenderness Interview, as recorded at http://speakingoffaith.publicradio.org/programs/wisdomoftenderness/.

is a whole-of-life approach, enabling people to grow in trust, to want to become a follower of Christ. This is easy to say, but it might take people many years to face their anger, pain and egos. In conversion, we encounter the vulnerability of Christ, and the Gospel stories where Christ himself was rejected, because change was sometimes too difficult. So pre-discipleship and catechesis are crucial and have to be contextual, opening up orthopraxis as an approach to faith, if it is going to be authentic. In this approach, conversion and formation seek to help people shift from being unchurched explorers to becoming Christian pilgrims.

Concerning discipleship and catechesis following conversion, some new monastic groups have developed approaches that engage with the dual tracks of the inward journey of spiritual formation and the outward journey of social transformation and action. This dual approach then resonates with the focus on the question *How should we live?* which is about orthopraxis. Formation is beyond knowing a list of facts about God, it must encompass inner spiritual formation and outer, servant-hearted social transformation.

So new monastics have been experimenting with a particular approach to formation with never-churched people who are wanting to dig deeper with the Christian faith. We might summarize it in this way:

1. A whole-of-life approach is therefore taken towards discipleship/catechesis, not unlike novices of monastic communities. A focus on learning through intentional community and belonging, with different expectations of levels of commitment regarding a rhythm of life, spiritual practices, virtues and postures.

2. A balanced approach to study, exploration and participation in loving service as formation.

3. Focus on learning through experience of life, through reflective and prayerful formation.

4. Use of mentors and spiritual directors to assist people to explore the faith through an individual inspirational and facilitatory approach. It is less about learning abstract facts about

God through an apologetic approach (argument and concept), and more about learning through experience of God through spiritual encounter and service.

5. Emphasis on a contemplative experience and the discernment of God who is already present in life, rather than an approach of accepting God into your life. Conversion, then, is less about accepting a conceptual framework concerning God to be true, and more about a transformation of the heart, and experiencing God to be true in life.

6. Emphasis on incarnational theology. Many people do not know who they are, but know they have a need for God. This approach assists people to grow in an understanding of grace and the love of God, to know that we have a need for God which helps us to face our brokenness and our need to grow, becoming more human.

7. Discipleship is countercultural. It is not about choice as consumptive gratification, about belonging to a spiritual club and getting your ticket to heaven, but rather emphasizes the cost of discipleship and following Christ as the passionate life – one that celebrates all that is good in life, but one also that leads to the cross, pain and suffering.[4]

These seven points resonate with an approach recommended by Pete Ward, who encouraged youth workers to utilize a more 'practical theology' to working with younger people, where social context and reflective learning through experience are coupled with discipleship.[5] In this form, we need to look at discipleship as more like the model of 'learning on the job', an apprenticeship scheme, rather than a more intellectual approach of engaging with logical or apologetic argument to synthesize personal belief. So an apprenticeship approach to discipleship in the context of community which is about contemplation and action resonates with a number of new monastic communities, and indeed the novitiate of ancient Christian monasticism.

---

4 This summary is drawn from compiling interviews with leaders of new monastic communities and from reading of a number of new monastic books.

5 Pete Ward, 2008, *Participation and Mediation: A Practical Theology for the Liquid Church*, Norwich: SCM Press.

To examine this more fully, we will explore a number of approaches utilized by new monastic communities on both sides of the Atlantic.

Most of the communities we will look at have defined different spaces of learning, action and commitment, symbolically using the image of an onion to describe this. Discipleship is focused on the idea of spiritual formation as growing into Christlikeness.

The UK 24–7 Boiler Rooms

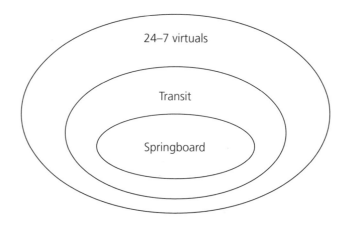

The 24–7 Boiler Rooms, now an international new monastic community, takes a structured approach to discipleship. Their main vehicle for formation is what they have called '24–7 Transit', facilitating three levels of discipleship and learning, as seen in the diagram above.

> It is worth thinking about these courses like an onion. Some, like 24–7 virtual can be found on the outer layer – a chance even if you're a long way away, to get some of the values and theology of 24–7 prayer into your discussion. Some, like Transit, can be found a few layers in – providing a chance for first-time learning, but also a chance to meet people face-to-face, spend time with the movement, and see where God takes you. Finally,

there are courses, like Springboard, at the core of the movement – asking you to commit two years to a mix of learning and
mission in a Boiler Room around the world.[6]

Like traditional monasticism, they take their starting place for
formation in the Transit scheme, from the great commandment
and the great commission, in three distinct areas:

1. Authentic spirituality (equipping you to be true to Christ):
   'You shall love the Lord your God with all your heart' (Luke
   10.27).
2. Relational spirituality (equipping you to be kinder to
   people): 'You shall love your neighbour as yourself' (Luke
   10.27).
3. Missional spirituality (equipping you to take the gospel to
   the world): 'Go and make disciples of all nations' (Matthew
   28.19).[7]

Those individuals who join the Transit scheme live in some form
of intentional community for ten months, with a focus on three
principles: work, rest and prayer.

24–7 is committed to a learning philosophy that develops mind,
body and spirit in the context of practical action as well as more
formal 'classroom' settings. This model of experiential learning
works on three distinct levels, relating to the three foci of the great
commandment and great commission:

1. The Living Room – Students will live together and therefore
   share life together. It is in this environment that students will
   learn what it means to put the theory of loving one another
   into practice and be discipled together in community. All
   students will also receive personal mentoring which focuses
   on issues of character development, support and ongoing
   discipleship.

---

6 http://www.24-7prayer.com/learning (accessed 6 January 2010).
7 http://www.24-7prayer.com/learning/transit-syllabus (accessed 9 January 2010).

2. The Boiler Room – Students belong to a small team (maximum 12) based with a 24-7 Boiler Room in either the UK or the USA. In this context, they get to practise a rhythm of work, rest and prayer as part of a missional community actively engaged with the poor and the lost. This is one of the things that makes Transit unlike so many theory-driven courses: you're learning by doing.

3. The Classroom – Students gather together in a classroom setting to interact with an amazing array of teachers and practitioners at regular times throughout the year. During these more formal teaching times, we also take time to walk through a programme we call 'God's Story' – a ten-month overview of the Bible which is consistently voted the most popular aspect of Transit. Students are also given reading and writing assignments as part of their study time.[8]

For all those who enter the Transit programme, the great commission and great commandment listed above is broken down into a three-part rule which it calls the 'Order of the Mustard Seed', summarized as:

Practically, Transit identifies these dimensions with the triune vow of the Order of the Mustard Seed:

1. Be True to Christ in Prayer, Worship, Intercession, Creativity and the Arts.
2. Be Kind to All People through Mercy, Social Justice, Hospitality, the Family and Lifestyle.
3. Take the Gospel to All Nations through Mission and God's Strategy for History through Training, Making Disciples.[9]

Transit, then, takes participants through a form of conversion, with a structured whole-of-life approach to spiritual formation, to enable young people to become committed Christian disciples.

---

8 http://www.24-7prayer.com/learning/transit-model (accessed 8 January 2010).
9 http://www.24-7prayer.com/learning/transit-syllabus (accessed 8 January 2010).

From conversations with those involved in 24–7 Boiler Room communities, this form of discipleship and formation has been highly effective. The emphasis on discovering God practically through life and a rhythm of life has been the right focus.

In the Transit Classroom, students receive ten months of learning called the 'God Story', which is an entire overview of the Bible regarding salvation history and an understanding of the faith. According to 24–7, God Story has been highly effective because it ties in learning with action and communal living.[10]

Andy Freeman, one of the co-founders of this new monastic community, described their approach to knowledge, saying learning the story about God as a narrative has been important. Here the Bible is interpreted as being a guide.

The book that 24–7 are using as a basis for this formation is Philip Greenslade's *God's Story Through the Bible Promise by Promise*. This approach is significant, because narrative storytelling has become an important conveyer of meaning in postmodern and post-secular cultures.

Martyn Percy, Principal of Ripon College Cuddesdon and Honorary Professor of Theological Education at King's College London, affirms the need for this approach:

The relationship between words and images has changed in contemporary culture. In a post-foundational world, it is the power of the image that takes us to the text. The Bible is no longer a principal source of morality, functioning as a rule-book. The gradualism of postmodernity has transformed the text into a guide, a source of spirituality, in which the power of the story as but one potential moral reference point has superseded the didactic. Thus the meaning of the Good Samaritan is more important than the Ten Commandments – even assuming the latter could be remembered in any detail by anyone. Into this milieu the image speaks with power.[11]

---

10 http://www.24-7prayer.com/learning/transit-syllabus (accessed 8 January 2010).
11 Martyn Percy, 1998, *The Salt of the Earth: Religious Resilience in a Secular Age*, London: Continuum, p. 165.

The God Story learning event has 36 sessions working through the whole of salvation history; the titles are summarized below:[12]

- Introduction to the God Story
- The Beginning – Genesis 1—2
- The Fall – Genesis 3—4
- Abraham – Genesis 12—22
- Isaac and Jacob – Genesis 23—36
- Joseph and Moses – Genesis 37–Exodus 13
- The Exodus – Exodus 14—36
- Wanderings and a New Generation – Leviticus 16–Deuteronomy 12
- Joshua – Deuteronomy 17–Joshua 24
- Judges – Judges 1—21
- Samuel and David – 1 Samuel 1–1 Kings 4
- Solomon and the Divided Kingdom – 1 Kings 6—15
- The Fall of the Northern Kingdom – 1 Kings 16–Hosea 6
- The Southern Kingdom – Jonah 1–2 Kings 25
- The Spirit of the Prophets – Daniel 1–Isaiah 58
- Life in Exile – Isaiah 60–Ezra 5
- The Return – Haggai 1–Malachi 4
- The Incarnation of Jesus
- How do we see Jesus?
- The Beatitudes
- The way of Jesus
- The Passion of Jesus
- The Resurrection and Pentecost
- Judea and Samaria: The Mystery Unfolds
- Paul's Missionary Journeys
- Paul's letter to the Roman Church
- Paul's letter to the Corinthian Church
- Paul's Final Journey
- Paul's Prison letters
- Paul's letters to Timothy
- Hebrews

---

12 http://kcboilerroom.com/the-god-story.

- Peter and John
- The Revelation of Jesus.

Students are encouraged to take this biblical learning into their experiences of loving service, community and personal spirituality. As people grow in formation, and attend different learning schemes, they grow into owning the full rhythm of life and spiritual practices of the wider community. The success of this approach is shown by the exponential growth of this new monastic community in both the USA and Europe.

The Sojourner covenant approach

The Church of the Sojourners in San Francisco takes a very similar path to 24–7 Boiler Room communities, again with an onion-layer approach to belonging, action and formation. Initial evangelism occurs in loving service to the local neighbourhood. Where people show an interest in the Christian faith, they are invited to join in with a structured programme, enabling people to grow in conversion through attending a whole-of-life approach to discipleship and catechesis.

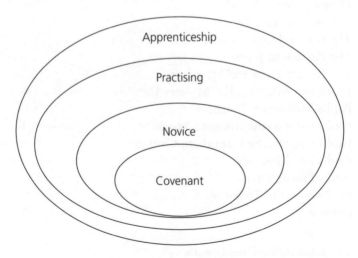

Starting with apprenticeship, discipleship begins with an approach to the faith owing much to covenant theology:

'you are a chosen people, a royal priesthood, a holy nation, God's own people, that you may declare the praises of him who called you out of darkness into his wonderful light', 1 Peter 2.9.

We remember that God covenanted with us, not because of any merits of ours, or because we are great in number or gifts, but rather he chose us to be his own people because he loves us ... Though he was God, he made himself nothing and became a slave. We forgive when we are sinned against and accept the pain it causes, knowing that we too are sinners.

We pledge faithfulness to God's economy: that economy where authority is revealed in servanthood and loves its way rather than forces its way. An economy where strength is shown in weakness. Where the poor are blessed and the rich are made low. Where God chooses the weak and powerless to be his royalty in order to demonstrate his glory. An economy that is foolishness to the world around us. We do not struggle to satisfy our own needs but to give ourselves away because we are fully supplied by God.[13]

With this starting point, the Church of the Sojourners draws its focus on discipleship and formation from covenant belonging:

Covenanting and living in covenant with others has been a centerpiece of the people of God. This feature is important to our understanding of what it means to form the kind of life together where we expect to grow old with one another. Our covenant is our way of giving each other permission that we will talk about major life decisions as a group. It affirms that we believe God to be at work redeeming the world through

---

13 http://churchofthesojourners.wordpress.com/living-church-family-style/our-covenant/ (accessed 8 January 2010).

his Church, that our true citizenship is in his kingdom, and that we at Sojourners experience that primarily in this church. Becoming a member of this church means to become a person for whom this covenant seems natural.[14]

Looking at the Sojourner community's process, discipleship begins at the apprenticeship stage. Here individuals are expected to commit a year of their time, living in a flat with other apprentices, learning to live as a community, sharing food, money, work, loving service, study, attending church events and shared governance.[15]

Each apprentice is appointed a mentor to assist with reflective learning, and to direct them in their developing understanding of the Christian faith and discipleship. At the end of the year, each apprentice is invited to continue in their formation by entering into the practising posture. This is for people who are not yet ready to enter into the commitments expected for the covenant level of belonging. All people involved in the community are able to participate within the wider new monastic community, but with different levels of commitment.

For those ready to enter into the covenant posture, this begins with a year's introduction to grow into this level of giving and belonging, which is called the novice posture. After this novice year, individuals are invited to enter into the covenant posture, which is about full belonging and committed engagement at the heart of the community.

At each stage, individuals are given the choice to continue developing their level of belonging, or pause at the level of practising, without necessarily committing to a deeper level. As we explored in an earlier chapter, there is real danger of developing a 'two-speed' community, causing problems if not handled carefully.

Both the 24-7 and Sojourner processes could become very controlling and institutional if not managed well. As long as the

14 http://churchofthesojourners.wordpress.com/living-church-family-style/membership-postures/ (accessed 8 January 2010).

15 http://churchofthesojourners.wordpress.com/living-church-family-style/membership-postures/ (accessed 8 January 2010).

process continues to be based on individual choice, participation and inspiration, then there is less possibility of control.

To work successfully, such forms of discipleship must be very relational, as they demand a high level of countercultural commitment.

Contemplative Fire

The Contemplative Fire communities in the UK and Canada are committed to promoting learning and formation with de- and unchurched people through a whole-life approach:

> The theology of the Trinity under-girds Contemplative Fire, and finds expression in the interconnectedness of being, knowing and doing; prayer, study and action. This is symbolised in the Celtic knot or trefoil.

A LEARNING JOURNEY
Equipping, exploring and accompanying others

STILL WATERS
Encountering the present moment in quietness

ACROSS THE THRESHOLD
Engaging with wisdom on the boundaries

Like the communities we have looked at thus far, Contemplative Fire also combines intentional community, teaching, contemplative prayer and worship with action.

> Through the use of the creative imagination in encountering texts and traditions, signs and symbols, through contemplative

chant, through inspirational teaching and with the support of travelling companions, those of us who choose to become members of the community – companions on the Way – will find ourselves drawn ever more consciously into the presence of God here and now. Those who feel called to hold in creative tension contemplation and action and who are becoming involved in the Contemplative Fire movement as members will be able to engage in one or more small communities of practice.[16]

Contextually, Contemplative Fire is working with a very different social grouping to 24–7 and Sojourners, which tends towards older, more artistically inclined spiritual seekers. Discipleship in this context requires less of a high commitment to attending a programme, and more of a commitment to quest with a particular small community of practice attending to the needs of the shared rhythm of life. Here, being part of a community is less about participation in an intentional community living together, and more about being part of a dispersed community living intentionally.

safespace

safespace is located in Telford, a new town not far from the border between England and Wales. Like many contexts in the UK, a formal course learning approach to discipleship will not work – and reflects a dislike for anything that feels like school. This creates a particular challenge in approaching formation for those who are not Christian.

Mark Berry, the community's lay pioneer minister, says they have chosen a more informal discussion and 'soul friends' approach. People are motivated by exploring life issues, and then reflecting on the implications concerning God and humanity. As Mark said:

---

16 http://www.contemplativefire.org/journey.htm (accessed 8 January 2010).

People are really wanting to talk about the difficult issues of life such as relationships, justice, broken relationships, sexuality, addiction, suffering and spiritual practices. These discussions always lead to questions about 'What is God?' and issues of faith. By wrestling through these questions in the context of community, people seek for where God is in life, to understand God in context, which opens up applied theology. So it is discipleship explored in the context of life experience, and is therefore an approach based on orthopraxis.[17]

This more open approach is a cultural response to the context. As with other new monastic communities, safespace has a high view of community as an interpretative community, assisting individuals in growing in their understanding and formation. This is reflected in the community's spiritual disciplines:

Our community rhythm of life:
Daily – scripture, meditation and prayer (including being surprised by God in ordinary life).
Weekly – fellowship, communion, accountability (weekly common table).
Seasonal – festival, celebration (marking 'holy days' and the rhythm of the earth).
Annual – pilgrimage (period of retreat and reflection on the year gone, the moment we are in and the year ahead).
Lifelong – learning, study.[18]

safespace is also a dispersed community, living locally and with a strong sense of calling to Telford. safespace has attempted to compensate for the challenge of not living in one residential space by encouraging regular community gatherings where people spend significant time together. Honesty and openness are an expectation, so participants learn about themselves and God through these times of relational intimacy. safespace also does a lot of

---

17 Transcript of telephone conversation between the authors, 8 January 2010.
18 Mark Berry (2007), *Navigatio*, London: Proost. www.proost.co.uk.

outreach to the community. At one 'Table' gathering they read John 4 (where Jesus meets the Samaritan woman at the well) and this inspired them to begin a Night-life ministry called Sank•tuary, a night cafe and street work which helps people who are drunk and under the influence of drugs.

> The idea for Sank•tuary came late in 2008 to the Telford community safespace whilst they were studying the story of Jesus meeting with a Samaritan woman told in John 4. Their discussions one cold December evening led them to the question: how did Jesus get there? Jesus had been travelling from Judea to Galilee. The usual route for Jews would have been to cross the River Jordan but Jesus chose to travel directly through Samaria. He stopped at a well at the hottest time of the day when everyone would normally be resting indoors. But the Samaritan woman he met was a social outcast who had been married five times and was not married to her current partner, so she chose to draw water at the time when no one else would be around.

> Jesus went to that well at that time to meet her. Most people would have thought that she wasn't worth giving the time of day to. The same is said of many young adults today who drink excessively; 'it's their own fault', 'they're not worth helping', 'they won't remember any of it in the morning'. safespace came to the conclusion that we can either judge these young people, or like Jesus, we can go out and help them and in small ways try to bring about a change in their lives. So following discussions with Telford and Wrekin Council, West Mercia Police and the Wellington Methodist Church a partnership was formed and just 3 weeks after the initial idea was raised Sank•tuary was open![19]

A number of those who have become volunteers at Sank•tuary are young people who have no relationship with church, but who feel that their lives are somehow missing something. One of the young

---

19 http://sanktuary.org.uk.

men who came into the cafe in its early days was a long-term drug addict. Over a year he became part of the team, giving him a sense of purpose and meaning and eventually he was able to stop taking drugs and find permanent work. Giving in this way helps spiritual seekers to encounter God through the generosity and love of the 'community in action'.

The Moot community

Moot specifically attempts to engage with un- and de-churched people who are interested in spirituality, justice and community. For the Moot community, the point of formation begins with people interacting with members of the community, in the hope that they will experience a loving and caring Christian and spiritual community through the Host Cafe they have built in the Guild Church of St Mary Aldermary in the City of London. Encountering such a community often seems to break down negative stereotypes and experiences that many people hold. Moot offers people two very different starting places. The first is the pub spirituality discussion group called 'Serum' which opens up the Christian faith through the exploration of issues. The second combines an introduction to spiritual practices such as meditation and prayer, while opening up the Christian faith in the context of spirituality. This is aimed at those who are seeking spiritually enriching experiences. Every week, the community holds a meditation group to engage with spiritual seekers living or working in the City of London.

Through the weekly meditation group and Serum people are offered experiential and conceptual approaches for questing with the Christian faith.

Those who want to join the community to explore faith more deeply, or those who want to commit to the community because they have found faith, are currently encouraged to attend a short course exploring the elements of Moot's rhythm of life. The rhythm of life encapsulates an aspiration of how to live in a way that opens up Christianity in the context of the everyday

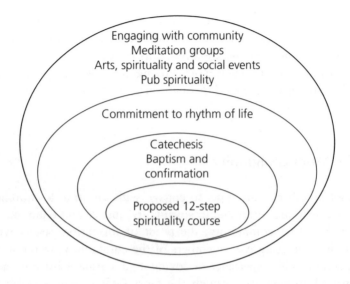

Engaging with community
Meditation groups
Arts, spirituality and social events
Pub spirituality

Commitment to rhythm of life

Catechesis
Baptism and
confirmation

Proposed 12-step
spirituality course

rather than abstract philosophical or theological thought. The short course includes an opportunity to explore the spiritual disciplines, virtues and postures of the community, opening up the landscape of Christian discipleship as a whole-of-life pursuit.

Committing to the rhythm of life happens through an annual service before the Bishop of London in keeping with the ancient practice of priests, monastics and friars recommitting to their vows in the season of Easter. Committing to the rhythm of life is a declaration of belonging to the heart of the Moot community; joining the electoral roll of the community enables people to vote and contribute at monthly governance meetings.

A further stage of formation is offered which resonates with Anglican–Episcopal church polity concerning the preparation for baptism or confirmation. Here a short course explores the baptismal covenant within this tradition, in the context of the Apostles' Creed.

Finally, the Moot community are piloting a new approach to catechesis through the combination of a 12-step course exploring Christian spirituality and practice and the 'I am' statements of Jesus in the Gospel of John. It is hoped that this combination will open up the themes of conversion, healing and formation, seeking to combine a relational accountability to dig deep, explore knowledge about the Christian faith, with prayerful meditation and action. Moot hope this will have an inspirational and transformational focus opening up the community's rhythm of life in life-changing ways.

Soul Spark

Returning again to the issue of combining learning content and experience (particularly for dispersed new monastic communities who do not have intentional community contexts to use for discipleship formation), new monastic communities have been exploring other resources. One worth noting is Soul Spark, a short course exploring prayer and spiritual growth created by Nick Helm.[20] This approach to formation through experience draws on the contemplative tradition, exploring faith through prayer.

The course is divided into six sessions consisting of some form of prayer exercise and then reflection in groups. These sessions are:[21]

Session	Title	Prayer Exercise
1	Approaching Spirituality	Praying with Scripture (*Lectio Divina*)
2	Journeying with God	Reflection Exercise
3	Who am I?	Praying with Scripture: Imaginative Contemplation
4	Who is God to me?	Visual Contemplation
5	Called to Become	Healing Prayer
6	Where am I Going? Journeying on ...	Poetry

20 Nick Helm, 2006, *Soul Spark: A Short Course Exploring Prayer and Spiritual Growth*, Cambridge: Grove Booklets.
21 Helm, *Spark*, p. 5.

These sessions are organized into the following structured session plan:[22]

Section	Timing
Welcome, Introduction and Check-In	10 mins
Stilling and Prayer Exercise	30 mins
Listening Groups	25 mins
Reflection on Listening Groups	7 mins
Input – reflections on subject	25 mins
Final reflection	10 mins

Offering this type of experiential course opens up the beginnings of a discipleship course without having to lose the non-propositional focus to this approach, where it is hoped that people will find the spiritual content of the course to be transformational, and therefore motivated to keep going.

While we are increasingly convinced that there is no possible replacement for the strength of a residential community for a depth of formation, for some new monastics, due to their context, this just isn't possible. For most new monastics, the luxury of a very large house to accommodate a community, either in whole or in part, is not possible, so dispersed communities are a reality, and for some, preferred. So approaches such as Soul Spark are a useful resource to engage with discipleship formation.

Reflections

As we explored earlier, new monastics have recovered an approach to formation based on experience and practice as a form of experiential apprenticeship. This is in many ways a recovery of the ancient catechumenate, the form of discipleship used in the early

---

22 Helm, *Spark*, p. 5.

church. The essential ingredients of participation in intentional community, costly loving service, experiential learning, contemplative prayer, meditation and whole-of-life learning, draw on a deep approach inherited through the wider monastic and friar traditions. Communities such as the 24–7 Boiler Rooms have shown that when this is facilitated well, it can be a very powerful approach to discipleship and Christian formation for contemporary never-churched people.

This whole-of-life form of discipleship crucially starts with a focus on *monos*, being alone, facing who you really are in a culture addicted to not facing the 'self'. Facing your pains, your brokenness, your shadow side is an important starting place for 'conversion' that will lead into discipleship and catechesis.

John O'Donohue summarizes the importance of this communitarian and whole-of-life approach to formation:

> If we become addicted to the external, our interiority will haunt us. We will become hungry with a hunger no image, person or deed can still. To be wholesome, we must remain truthful to our vulnerable complexity. In order to keep our balance, we need to hold the interior and exterior, visible and invisible, known and unknown, temporal and eternal, ancient and new, together. No-one else can undertake this task for you. You are the one and only threshold of an inner world. This wholesomeness is holiness ... When you cease to fear your solitude, a new creativity awakens in you. Your forgotten or neglected inner wealth begins to reveal itself. You come home to yourself and learn to rest within. Thoughts are our inner senses. Infused with silence and solitude, they bring out the mystery of the inner landscape.[23]

Christian formation begins with this individual spiritual journey that helps people to understand their own inner story. Their story is supported and nurtured through God's own story as they

---

23 John O'Donohue, 1997, *Anam Cara: Spiritual Wisdom from the Celtic World*, London: Bantam, pp. 14, 17.

experience it through their lives and spiritual community. The important place of the ecclesial community regarding individual formation births an understanding of being Christian, something the next chapter will explain.

10

Building real Community

The renewal of both the Church and Society will come through the re-emergence of forms of Christian community that are homes of generous hospitality, places of challenging reconciliation and centres of attentiveness to the living God.

Brother Samuel SSF[1]

Community=Mission

For Brother Samuel of Hilfield Friary in Dorset, community is not a place from which mission flows, rather the community is the mission itself. What does this mean? Well, it is easy to see our churches and communities like the missionary societies of yesteryear, as sending bodies from which we reach out into the wider community. Like the probably apocryphal story of the church which put a sign on the inside of the main door which read, 'Tradesman's entrance'. Church is the place from which mission flows, the place where we are resourced to go in mission and the place to which we come back to be resourced. But for new monastic communities, a depth of community is vital not only to sustain the ministry, but to be the locus for mission and evangelism. In other words, for many the community *is* the mission. This means the community is not only a place of sending, it is itself sent. David Bosch the South African missiologist in his seminal work, *Transforming Mission*, writes:

The classical doctrine on the missio Dei as God the Father sending the Son, and God the Father and the Son sending the Spirit was expanded to include yet another 'movement': The Father,

---

1 Taken from a podcast – mootuk.podbean.com.

Son and the Holy Spirit sending the church into the world. As far as missionary thinking was concerned, this linking with the doctrine of the Trinity constituted an important innovation ... Mission is thereby seen as a movement from God to the world; the church is viewed as an instrument for that mission. There is church because there is mission, not vice versa. To participate in mission is to participate in the movement of God's love toward people, since God is a fountain of sending love.[2]

The Church is drawn into the mission of the Trinity, drawn into this movement which Bosch details. The Church itself is sent, the community is the mission, participating in the mission of God, through the Son, with the Spirit. So the Church is both the agent of God's mission in the world and the fruit of God's mission in the world.

Seeking to engage with this characteristic of sent-ness, means asking hard questions about the nature of community – how do we live together, practise transparency, justice, humility, vulnerability and forgiveness.

safespace say about themselves:

We see the community as itself an embodiment of the Kingdom inwardly and outwardly. We seek to reflect shalom between ourselves. The community is a small but rich tapestry of Christian expression and churchmanship. In many ways we are post-denominational, we actively allow space for different views and interpretations of the Christian faith in the context of relationship and community. In many ways we believe that part of our charism is to celebrate unity in diversity, to model community rather than club or niche expression. As we live our lives in the wider community we seek to be people of shalom, to begin first by offering peace and by living in the wider community as opposed to 'reaching out' into it. In a culture where family and community are strained and struggling we believe a major part of a missional response is to model real community and love.

---

2 David J. Bosch, 1991, *Transforming Mission*, Maryknoll, NY: Orbis Books, pp. 389–90.

How we live together in the culture is as much a part of God's mission as the projects and things we do. New monastic communities are aware of this and work hard to find ways which help their members to reflect on how they encounter and hear God's call in everyday living and on how they live together as they 'move into the neighbourhood'. Rene Padilla, leading South American theologian, emeritus president of the Kairos Foundation, a Christian service agency whose raison d'être is to facilitate the reflection on and the practice of integral mission on the part of local churches, writes: 'The Incarnation unmistakably demonstrates God's intention to make himself known from within the human situation. Because of the very nature of the gospel, we know it only as a message contextualized in culture.'[3]

Some examples of different forms of new monasticism

Some new monastic communities are dispersed networks of lay people in a particular city or place. Some, such as the Earlsfield Friary, are a network of intentional households and some, such as the All Hallows Community in Bow, are an intentionally residential community after taking over a large clergy house. Most maintain a deep daily intentionality through liturgies and prayers that are shared during the day through various media: daily liturgies, emails, text messages, podcasts and other information technology. All have regular gatherings and most involve frequent community meals.

In *New Monasticism as Fresh Expression of Church* Ian describes new monastic communities in three ways:

> The first group, inspired by monks and nuns who have established new places for prayer and contemplation, gathering communities of people for worship and loving action in the local community with the de- and never-churched ... The

3 Rene Padilla, 1985, *Mission Between the Times*, Grand Rapids, MI: Eerdmans, p. 83.

second group of new monastics identify with the friar tradition. They are also committed to seeking the sacred in the ordinary but follow a different model. While the first group tends to gather for worship and action, and then disperse back to their homes, away from the meeting place, this second group tends to move into an area either as single households of pioneers or as intentional communities ... there is also a third group, which has a vision that combines both the monk and friar models.[4]

Communities of monks

The Northumbria Community

The Northumbria Community can trace its roots back to the 1970s. In 1989 the Nether Springs Trust, which had been set up to support the spiritual direction ministry of John Skinner, came together with Northumbria Ministries, a group committed to mission in Northumbria, led by Roy Searle. Out of this the Northumbria Community was formed. The community came to fruition in the mid-nineties when the Community Council was brought together.

The Northumbria Community is a dispersed community but with a strong connection to the ancient kingdom of Northumbria and island of Lindisfarne. As a dispersed community much of its focus has been to provide resources for members who then locate their spiritual practice and mission where they are.

> As a Community we have been – and are – united in the quest for 'a new monasticism': a Northumbrian spirituality. Not as an escapist, nostalgic quest for a golden era that didn't exist, or to replicate the past, but informed by the Celtic monastic tradition which is our heritage. We are 'looking with them to Him who inspires us both' in order to find a way to engage with the paradox and complexities of real life as it is.

4 Graham Cray, Ian Mobsby and Aaron Kennedy, 2010, *New Monasticism as Fresh Expression of Church*, Norwich: Canterbury Press, p. 13.

New monasticism, as in any expression of Monasticism, stands in the wisdom tradition – which is not an accumulation of knowledge for its own sake, but a constant application to life actually lived. 'A wise person does not gather and dispense insights, but rather has the heart to live those insights.'

Strongly influenced by the way of life expressed in the Monastic Communities at Roslin in Scotland and at Clonfert in Ireland; God's call on the Northumbria Community is not to any form of institutionalism but to embrace, explore and express the heart of monastic spirituality in the everyday ordinariness of our lives, as a different way of living in and relating to, today's world.

We do this by drawing from the well of faith and love for the Lord expressed in that period of our history, and applying it to our contemporary situation. We believe that we are experiencing as a Community (along with many others) a 'holy restlessness' and a 'divine concern' regarding the nature of faith, which has only begun to make sense of the nonsense within us and around us through an embracing of monastic values and disciplines.

Monastic spirituality implies a single-hearted (solitary) seeking of God. This may or may not be carried out in the company of others (the monastic tradition has embraced both alone and together), but the focus is clearly on returning to God, and making use of a daily rhythm of prayer (Office) and a Way for living (Rule), that enable us to 'marry' the inner journey, the landscape of the heart – a call to repentance, to self denial, and a call to recognise and to resist evil – with the outer journey, the landscape of the land, which has given us a platform to 'find a different way' of being Church. Then to offer the fruit of our life with all who come our way and cross our path in the every-dayness of our roles, responsibilities and relationships – asking with them 'Who is it that you seek? How then shall we live? How shall we sing the Lord's song in a strange land?'[5]

5 http://www.northumbriacommunity.org.

The strength of the Northumbria Community is that they create a context of community which helps members who are dispersed to reflect together on their calling to mission and community through the hub of a mother house. They have had to work hard to find ways which create a sense of connection with shared liturgies and reflections through a common prayer book. Many of these resources are rooted in an attempt to recover practices from the past. This therefore not only helps members appreciate the connectivity with other members but also the ancient and ongoing story of the monastic life and mission.

The Monos Community

Grown from roots within the Northumbria Community, Monos was launched in 2004. They describe themselves as,

> an inclusive and interdenominational Christian Organisation that is primarily focused on fostering a Christian Monastic spirit within the wider Christian Community and Society at large ... We are a community-based organisation that offers education to encourage the interest in spirituality, and in particular Monastic spirituality, amongst the Christian Church at large. Monos was developed, in order to provide a caring and educational facility for the on-going dialogue between Monastic spirituality, society, culture and church. And to begin to ask serious questions concerning the relationship between New/ Lay Monasticism, Church and society, both historically and contemporarily.[6]

The community runs a mother house with several centres as a resource for the Church, leading retreats and courses to encourage churches to think about monastic culture, spirituality and values. This is new monasticism as a resource to reconnect the Church to monastic spirituality as well as spiritual direction and reflection.

---

6 www.monos.org.uk.

Communities of friars

EarthAbbey

The idea of EarthAbbey was first explored in 2008. It began as a booklet which focused on creative ways of living ethically in creation. From there it has grown into a community which is connected largely through web-based resources and conversations. Indeed EarthAbbey's web content is in the form of a wiki which allows members to form the content.[7] The values are expressed as:

- The need to live more in tune with the earth – people of the future will look back on the twenty-first century and characterise it in terms of whether or not human beings learnt to live in a more harmonious way with the earth and its other creatures.
- The recognition that this will require a deep transformation of both our inner lives and our societies.
- The intention to draw on a hope found in the Judaeo-Christian faith of a peace that will come to embrace the whole creation.
- While recognising the specific calling of this age to engage with the issues presented by our relationship with the natural world, we also embrace established human concerns for justice in human relations and the need to listen and respond to the needs of the most disadvantaged people among us.

There is a clear focus on shaping a lifestyle which reflects a common ethic. It is likely that for most members this ethic is the primary reason for joining the community. While the values are perhaps broad enough to be inclusive and organic, there is a strong focus on environmental issues which might feel exclusive, this is reflected in the themes of their spiritual resources and practices. Nevertheless EarthAbbey do describe themselves as a prophetic community inspired by the life and mission of Jesus and there is a clear intent to grow a deeper and perhaps broader community around mission.

---

7 Wiki is a website resource which allows its users to add, modify or delete its content by a web browser.

We pursue a life-affirming, creative spirituality that is open to all. EarthAbbey is more than a website. It is a movement of people and you are invited to join.

The heart of the community is the life of the individual members and their annual reflection on their lives. This results in offers of help, and requests for help, from other members. Some of our members have particular projects that they are developing where the vision, skills, experience and labour of other members would be of value. Some people may need paying for the services that they offer to other members. That is OK and members should state what they need. We recognise the need to make livings, but we hope that many will also be able to offer some things on a voluntary, or mutual sharing, basis.

Some others may have particular ideas about how EarthAbbey might express its life and seek others to help them make that real, perhaps running a retreat or developing some devotional resources. Some may be willing to offer help with editing the public side of our website, which will become like our magazine, with inspirational content provided by members and publicity for members' projects.

We encourage members to share the story of their own projects. Private needs and struggles can be shared among members in the Cloister, while public announcements and story can be submitted to the 'magazine', or public part of the website. Members provide text and pictures for the 'magazine' and then an editor will shape it up and post it.

Some members will also form local Way of Life groups to encourage them on their journey. These are small groups of 4–6 people who meet in a home every other month for a period of 3–4 hours. At the meeting, each person in turn is given space to share reflections and goals on their Way of Life and the group responds, as in the action/learning model, with questions, but not comments, on what has been said. The group may also share food, and some devotional time if the members want that. The commitment to the group is for one year. Then it should be renegotiated.[8]

EarthAbbey shares a common identity with the Northumbria Community as a dispersed new monastic community. But Earth-Abbey grew from a lifestyle concern and a desire to explore and live a specific ethic, 'Encouraging one another to journey towards a life more in tune with the earth', rather than a broader desire for community built around a mother house. EarthAbbey has an extremely clear membership and formation process, including providing novices with an Anam Cara (Soul Friend) to help them reflect on who they are, what they bring to the community and on their 'way of life'.

The Order of Mission

Formed from the ministry of Mike Breen at St Thomas's Church in Sheffield, the Order of Mission grew from a church planting movement. Much of their practice is built around Breen's work on formation (Lifeshapes) and church planting. The Order is highly structured with a Chapter formed from all permanent members who elect the Senior Guardian, with a Rule of Life and Vows. They describe themselves as a community of 'Kingdom Leaders' and the journey to permanent membership takes four years.

The Order of Mission is inspired by the monastic movements of previous eras that have so often been the tip of the sword for revival and awakening in the church at large.

There seems to be wide recognition that we live in days of great upheaval. TOM is a pioneering movement born out of a desire to fully give ourselves to making disciples of Jesus in this ever-changing world. We stand in the tradition of the mission-ary communities of the past who lived as radical, pioneering

---

8 http://www.earthabbey.com.

pilgrims called to influence, serve and shape society and the church in their time: the Celtic monks and nuns who first re-evangelised these nations, the Methodists and the Salvation Army who called a people back to God in their days, the Protestant missionary societies who re-discovered global mission in the nineteenth century.

The Order of Mission is a dispersed community of leaders who have taken vows of simplicity, purity and accountability, as well as living out a rule of life. Some members of TOM find themselves in full-time vocational ministry, but much of our order are not paid to 'do' the work of Jesus. We are people called to lead and influence within whatever context and culture they live and work: cities and rural areas, developed and developing countries, business, education, arts, health and social care, public and private sector, family and church.[9]

There is a very strong attitude of mission in the Order, indeed the founding purpose is to impact the world. Many of the members are in full-time ministry within the Church, but they also see their calling as influencers and shapers in culture. Though they are a dispersed order, there is a very strong recognition of the importance of gathering regularly, both in small regional groups and at larger national and international gatherings.

Earlsfield Friary

Sitting in the heart of Wandsworth in south London, between Wimbledon and Clapham, Earlsfield is a typical south London suburb. It has a very diverse mix of creeds and cultures and is for many a stepping stone out of urban London as they move further away from the inner city.

The Friary community is based around five households who come together to explore how they can live out the Christian faith in practice:

---

9 http://www.missionorder.org.

We have a central rhythm of life, seeking to focus on our individual spirituality, work and home lives. We focus on 'mission life, discipleship and open community'. The Friary itself has four key values: 'mutual rhythm, mutual Christ, mutual support and mutual mission'. We are not into becoming a specific 'intentional community' living all together. Instead we seek to become a 'community of intention' by the way we choose to live as a network of people.

We gather weekly on Mondays for prayer and on Thursdays over a shared meal and to break bread together. We are very much linked into the Church in the local area too, with some of us worshipping at different services on Sunday mornings.

This model and practice of community across a number of households is one which is becoming more common. This is not a dispersed model nor is it a residential monastic community. Communities like Earlsfield Friary have a very strong sense of calling to the local and see themselves as highly located. Living in the area which they feel called to serve is crucial.

As we have looked at embracing a mission spirituality, we have landed on two things that are the essence of Jesus' own ministry. Though seemingly simple they have been profound in our own story. Jesus was committed to eating together with others, and healing people ... We are trying to help each creatively in how we practise a mission spirituality not only in our local area but also in the spheres of life we work in. We are talking about how to do this and what this looks like. How do we support each other if I am a stay at home Mum or Dad, work in the media industry, education, and so on?

Real transformation is dependent upon how we personalize change in our own walk of faith and allow for the person of Christ to both break and shape us into becoming our true self. It is in this process that all missional endeavours can embrace the importance of being salt and light. Salt to preserve the goodness of creation and resist a gravitational pull to rot. Light to open our eyes to see beyond the limitations of what we think we know.[10]

The particular spirituality of this kind of new monastic community holds together an intention to grow deeper in their relationships with each other, God and with the culture they live in, sharing a 'mutual rhythm, mutual Christ, mutual support and mutual mission'.

All Hallows Bow[11]

In 2010, Cris Rogers heard the story of the decay of the parish church of All Hallows Bow Road. The plan was to give up on this church building and the large estate where it was based. Instead, it was proposed, that the building become a mosque. The Bow Road housing estate like many other inner-city estates was increasingly a place for social exclusion and downward mobility. It had lost its self-respect, and become a sink-estate. So Cris and a number of friends proposed to the diocese that they plant a new missional community on the estate, and use the large clergy house for a number of families and individuals to draw together in a rhythm of daily prayer, worship and service.

Cris became the Associate Vicar of All Hallows Bow Road in Bromley by Bow, and a neo-monastic community was established. They began seeking to build a relational hub on the estate, and to open up the church building as a place to service the community and hold worship services. With the presence on the estate, they began to befriend many people, seeking to assist them and contribute to a sense of local community.

The church set up a cafe drop-in, and a number of social initiatives to encourage social cohesion, and the church community has now grown. This is a classic example of how a missional new monastic community has assisted a parish that had died to be revitalized, and where a new monastic model of church with a

10 http://www.freshexpressions.org.uk/stories/earlsfieldfriary.
11 www.allhallowsbow.org.uk.

daily rhythm of prayer, worship and service has catalyzed new life. This example shows why it is important that intentional community needs to be a focus, as out of the shared relationships of this house, a church community has been reborn. In the context of the housing estate, this community is now running discipleship and other programmes assisting people to become Christian or dig deeper with faith.

They regularly throw parties on the green in the estate by the church. During Easter 2012 they held a party called 'Love Wins' with tents and lots of activities including face painting, food and arts for young people run by younger Christians.

Communities of monk/friars

24–7 Boiler Rooms

24–7 prayer began in 1999 as an initiative to help young people develop creative prayer lives and to bring churches together in prayer.

> A season of 24–7 Prayer provides a place, a time, a context and a catalyst for prayer. It's a practical tool helping ordinary people to pray. Many who would consider themselves bad at praying turn up for their hour slot in a prayer room and then stay for two. One is rarely enough.

From this practice of resourcing prayer the vision to grow 24–7 communities, or Boiler Rooms, emerged. The 24–7 Boiler Room Community is interestingly a fusion of a monk and friar new monastic community. It began with prayerful discernment of two leading figures, Pete Greig and Andy Freeman, committed to mission and evangelism in Reading. At one of their many prayerful gatherings of the fledgling community they felt called to visit a derelict pub on the site of an ancient monastic community in Reading. This ex-pub quickly became a Boiler Room, a hub of activity for the community, who then held prayer gatherings with an openness to the guidance of the Holy Spirit to lead them into all sorts of activity. From the beginning the community had been specifically youth-focused, and the new Boiler Room soon became well known among local youth in the town. The Boiler Room had events going on in it all day (24–7!) most days of the week. It became a gathering point for many local young people where there were few local amenities or clubs for younger people to go to.

The walls of the Boiler Room became covered with art, and all sorts of expressions of prayer, with candles and installations. It literally gave people space to express and explore Christian spirituality through creativity. For many, this opened up the Christian faith in a completely new and relevant way. As many unchurched young people continued to gather, the Boiler Room became a place of pilgrimage and encounter with God. To support this growing new monastic community, they created a Boiler Room Rule which defined its two purposes, three principles and six spiritual practices.

In this model, the Boiler Room becomes a place of pilgrimage to practise worship and mission. Alongside this, a number of new households have been set up, intentional communities for young people to live together to grow into the faith through the practice of spiritual disciplines. This model then encompasses a Boiler Room for praxis and intentional living for formation. Six practices have been developed from the experience of Boiler Room living:

A Boiler Room is true to Christ by being:
- A prayerful community practising a daily rhythm which includes all kinds of prayers on all occasions.
- A creative community where artistic expressions of prayer and worship may take the form of art, sculpture, new music, poetry, dance, fun and a celebratory lifestyle.

A Boiler Room is kind to people by being:
- A just and merciful community where the practical needs of the local poor are met and where liberation is championed.
- A hospitable community where pilgrims are welcomed,

meals are shared and where friendships can flourish across boundaries of race and culture.

A Boiler Room is committed to taking the gospel to the world by being:

- A missional community existing for incarnation and proclamation of the gospel to all people. To act as well as to pray.
- A learning community of training and discipleship, where people are growing in their faith, their life-skills and their ability to lead.[12]

24–7 Boiler Rooms have sprung up in other towns and cities in the UK, on Continental Europe and in the United States. It has quickly grown into a fresh expression of monasticism and church for youth with an international perspective. The mother community in Reading continues to make an impact in the local area. Unfortunately, the community was required to move out of the Boiler Room ex-pub building, and now depends on activities in other community spaces, yet people seek to hold to the agreed spiritual practices concerning worship, mission and community.

safespace Telford

safespace was born as a partnership between the Diocese of Lichfield and the Church Mission Society. It began with two questions: 1. What might Christian community look like in a post-Church culture? and 2. What would it look like were it shaped by mission? What has emerged is described by the community as,

a community of followers who are seeking first and foremost to be equipped, resourced and supported in living a life that exudes mission, to reflect a mission and holistic spirituality and to live that life alongside those for whom church has no meaning or connection and to be focussed on being agents of transformation in the world in which we find ourselves.

---

12 http://uk.24-7prayer.com.

The community meets each week around the meal table:

> We make and eat a meal, we invite guests to join us, we spend time in reflection and meditation on Scripture, we write, create and use liturgy, we break bread and share wine together, we pray together and we gently and generously hold each other accountable. We have been surprised how vital it has been to eat together as family, with no 'head of the table', as equals and how real the breaking of bread and sharing of wine feels in this context. We have welcomed guests from all over the world and from other faiths to share and reflect with us on God, Spirituality, Mission and Community. We have all been surprised by the depth of spiritual reflection and the real sense of the presence of God in our midst and how guests have effortlessly slotted into our community gatherings.

From this time together have come a number of mission projects, including the Sank•tuary night ministry described in Chapter 7. The community see the table as both a place of hospitality and spirituality and the place from where mission flows, both in terms of new projects but also in the life of the community among those with whom they live and work. The Community use a simple weekly pattern for reflection:

- See and appreciate something new in Creation
- Explore something about Jesus
- Listen in silence to the Spirit
- Bless and be blessed by someone
- Listen to and share a God story with someone
- Pray for and ask for prayer from someone
- Rest.

Moot

The Moot community grew out of a commitment to build an ecclesial community aimed at spiritual seekers in London who did not relate to traditional or contemporary expressions of church. In the beginning the community formed from people who had been involved in alternative worship groups and emerging churches. So after meeting to pray and explore a way forward, the community began alternative worship services on Sunday evenings at a church building in Westminster in central London with discussion groups exploring Christian spirituality and arts-as-mission events in clubs, bars and art galleries.

Learning from the experiences of the Northumbria Community and the hOME community in Oxford, Moot began a process of forming its own rhythm of life over a year. Following a process of prayerful discernment, the Moot community sensed a calling to set up an arts cafe lounge and an intentional community mother house, in addition to the dispersed network community it had established. In 2011 Moot moved to the Guild Church of St Mary Aldermary, the oldest of the church buildings attributed to St Mary in the City of London and opened Host as an arts cafe and a centre for mission to post-secular spiritual seekers in the City.

Moot is another example of a form of new monasticism that fuses both monk and friar traditions. They seek to develop mission and community in a particular location (in the Bow Lane area of the City of London where many work) and in a relational network (of those who are either spiritual unchurched seekers or dechurched ex-Christians and live within the M25 motorway). Moot specifically aims to engage with those who are 'spiritual and not religious' who live in London or work in the City, many of whom perceive themselves as spiritually impoverished. The cafe and website act as hubs for the community to practise relational hospitality as a form of Christian mission.

Each new monastic community we have encountered has its own sense of purpose, vision and values. But there are increasingly common themes and practices within new monasticism which are beginning to help us understand how the movement relates to each other, to the Church and to traditional monasticism. What we learn from these different examples of new monastic communities is that each community has a clear sense of its own calling and of the context in which it works this out. Some had a clear sense of this before bringing the community into being, others took time in the early stages to work through what this means for them.

There are seven stages of pilgrimage and these can be reflected on as the new monastic community works out its calling.

1. What does it mean to journey together?
2. What are the signs that lead us on the journey?
3. Who are my companions, how much do I really know them?
4. What is the story of the people and places we walk?
5. How do we become part of the ongoing story of the community?
6. Where do we encounter moments where heaven and earth touch?
7. How do we develop our awareness of God in each other and all people?

It is too easy to see new monasticism as a romantic dream, but all of the communities above have had to ground their existence in reality and work out ways of being together framed by a common sense of calling and ultimately a love of God, of each other and of the community in which they find themselves. This can only happen through a faithful spirituality which seeks God's lead in all we do.

> The church is the 'I in them and you in me' community, the community of the Father, Son, and Holy Spirit. The Trinitarian existence of the church grounds the Christian community in Reality, the most fundamental of realities: God as source of life and being, Creator, providential Sustainer, and New-Creation-Bringer.[13]

---

13 Howard A. Snyder, 2002, *Decoding the Church: Mapping the DNA of Christ's Body*, Grand Rapids, MI: Baker Books.

11

Practising healthy Community

Christianity entered history as a new social order ... From the very begin-
ning Christianity was not primarily a 'doctrine', but ... a 'community'
... a New Community, distinct and peculiar ... to which members were
called and recruited ... Christians felt themselves to be closely knit
together ... in a unity which radically transcended all human boundaries
– of race, of culture, of social rank, and indeed the whole dimension of
'this world'.[1]

Functional and healthy spiritual community has been repeatedly identified as a crucial element of new monasticism regarding formation of individuals and participative action in life. In a culture focused on individual consumer gratification, being and growing into community is quite a challenge. As we have seen in previous chapters, this critically begins with the individual facing him- or herself, warts and all, in the context of a strong ecclesial community. Without a strong and healthy spiritual community, a whole-of-life approach to formation will not work.

The challenge is great. Many people today have grown up in an overly individualistic and narcissistic culture. So much so that many have impoverished interpersonal skills or awareness. So how do we build a deep interdependent community with people who only exist at the surface of themselves? Or, with people who do not know how to be friends with people they do not like? For starters, we need to understand people will need to painfully acquire these necessary skills.

Building this type of community needs to begin with an explicit rhythm of life, spiritual practices, virtues and postures which act

---

1 G. Florovsky in B. A. Harvey, 1999, *Another City*, Harrisburg, PA: Trinity Press International, pp. 21–2.

as a guide and ground rules. This framework creates the environment not only to experience and be sustained by God, but also for the practical need of interpersonal skills acquisition. As an aside, even clergy in their ministerial training are not taught how to do this. It is a real need for all those involved in servant leadership to know how to develop group skills and how to facilitate such groups. Developing such skills is crucial for pioneers. For this reason, ministers of churches have much to learn from youth workers whose work is centred on this. Fortunately one of us trained as a youth worker before becoming a pioneer new monastic and the other trained as an occupational therapist, and was taught how to lead therapeutic groups. Had either of us not had this training, we would never have been able to perform the function of new monastic leaders.

Building such an ecclesial community among people with all sorts of issues and problems needs to begin with an agreed organizational framework with explicit 'expecteds', and with servant leaders who have good interpersonal and facilitatory skills.

Here, we hit the greatest strength and weakness of a new monastic model of church. In this form of church, people need to build closer and healthier relationships as a participative ecclesial community, which requires greater interpersonal skills and resilience than traditional expressions of church. Participants need to be very self-aware and importantly, be able to recognize when they have 'stuffed up' and be able to say sorry and face destructive patterns of behaviour when they occur. This is painful and not easy, and some who are attracted to this form of church may not be able to participate in it because of this lack of self-knowledge or ability to say sorry. There is a reason why St Benedict gave novices three opportunities to get it wrong and face up to it when they did.

This emphasizes the important need for new monastic communities to be deep and spiritually nourishing, beginning with individual *monos* – being alone and being able to face oneself with understanding – with a willingness to go deeper. In situations where individuals are unable to face themselves, one tends to find that people project their issues and insecurities (often

unconsciously) into the ecclesial community, which can result
in unhealthy and dysfunctional relationships. This is why some
churches feel so difficult to be part of, let alone to join. So the
building of community needs to begin with a commitment of individuals to go deeper and face themselves in the belief that God
loves them. Only then can a new ecclesial community be founded
in the DNA of love.

Our individual human identity does not begin with consumptive choice, but on the contrary, it begins with being instituted
by God and then constituted by relationships with other people.[2]
So self-identity and spiritual formation are deeply connected,
and when done well, constitution of identity can be enriched by
belonging to deep community. As Miroslav Volf has said:

> It is precisely the uniqueness of God's relation to me that makes
> me into a unique person. Yet in God's relation to me, a relation
> creating me as an individual human being, I do not stand as an
> individual isolated from other human beings and my environ-
> ment. An isolated individual of this sort does not exist. Human
> beings are in actuality imbedded in a network of multiple and
> diverse social and natural relationships: this applies not only to
> newborn infants, who have not yet become infants, who have
> not yet become subjects, but even to solitary ascetics, who do,
> after all, live a spiritually real communion and must draw their
> sustenance from nature ... God's own relationship with human
> beings, a relationship that first constitutes a human being into
> a person, always realizes itself through the differentiated exist-
> ence of every person in these multiple relations ... Without
> other human beings, even God cannot create a human being!
> Even if God were to create an isolated being, that being would
> not be a human being.[3]

Volf's argument underlines the importance of covenant theology
to underpin a healthy spiritual community. This starts with the

2 Ian Mobsby, 2007, *The Becoming of G–d*, Oxford: YTC Press, pp. 13–132.

3 Miroslav Volf, *After Our Likeness: The Church as the Image of the Trinity*,
Grand Rapids, MI: Eerdmans, pp. 182–3.

I–Thou covenant relationship between God and an individual instituting a sense of gift and responsibility regarding personal identity and being Christian. It also constitutes a covenant between the person and the spiritual community based upon the new commandment to love the Lord your God with all your heart, mind and strength, and love your neighbour as yourself. So the journey of building community begins with covenant, which lies at the heart of both Judaic and Christian thinking. A rhythm of life is, in effect, an expression of covenant to God in the context of a community with a focus on daily living.

Looking at the experience of a number of Christian new monastic and communitarian initiatives, we find a process with five stages necessary for the formation of a full and deep expression of ecclesial community, summarized in the table below.

FORMING AN ECCLESIAL COMMUNITY

START   MATURE

1	2	3	4	5
Love, Pain and Tenderness	Trust and Belonging	Forgiveness	Hope	Justice

Love, pain and tenderness

Community begins with the receiving and giving of love. At a very deep and primal level, we all long to be appreciated and loved. We carry a deep wound – the desire to be accepted and belong. Many of us have experienced expressions of love from our parents that have been either conditional or manipulative. This form of love leaves a wound deep within us. We can become wary of love, insecure and fearful of being vulnerable. So when people experience a spiritual community as being unconditionally loving, this often puts individuals in touch with their deep wound. At this early stage of joining a community, it is crucial that tenderness and gentleness are consistently experienced by new people from members of the host community. People at this stage need a lot of support in facing such inner pain. Often such individuals can become very hard on others, projecting such pain onto relationships, so loving pastoral support is important.

Developing a spiritually nourishing prayer and meditation life is important to enable people to experience the love of God as well as the love of a community, growing into the community's rhythm of life. In this way, formation and belonging to community go hand in hand.

Yet the expression of such unconditional love requires sacrifice and vulnerability, and recognizes the importance of free will – that is, that people may not choose to want to be loved. Here a community encounters the deep pain and vulnerability of God, who unconditionally loves us and gives us the freedom to reject that love. We encounter this pain when Jesus asks Peter in John's Gospel, *Do you love me?*

Jean Vanier described this as the cry and vulnerability of the loving God, the cry of all of us who are wounded. Community is formed when our cries and God's cry come together.[4] Community begins with a commitment to receiving and expressing love in relationships, where individual pain needs careful pastoral support, to help people to face their real inner selves, and to avoid projecting such pain onto communal relationships.

Where people experience immense pain after receiving unconditional love, care needs to be taken as it can trigger anxiety and depression. This is particularly true for those who have felt unwanted or ashamed of who they are. So individual transformation and formation coupled with the beginning of community helps people to experience grace – the love of God – in a profound, whole-of-life way. Communities that express tenderness reveal that all individuals in the community are loved. Gentleness and affirmation reveal to people that they are precious, and these give people dignity and value. By facing who we really are, we face our collective fragility, vulnerability, brokenness and our need for God, which then frees us to be able to express humility and love to others.

---

4 Jean Vanier interviewed by Krista Tippett on American Public Radio, http://speakingoffaith.publicradio.org/programs/wisdomoftenderness/.

Such new monastic communities are then able to offer loving service to the poor, sick and needy in costly support. Communities are then able also to grow in depth and in outward focus in countercultural ways that take people away from self-absorption and narcissism. This will not be an easy process, often requiring endurance and struggle.

Trust and belonging

In the development of community, what is needed next is trust. One of the greatest threats to healthy community is the inability to be able to listen and accept others. This is difficult when you do not like someone, and is made particularly harder when you live in close proximity to them. New monastic communities can be difficult places to be if you are working, worshipping and living with the same people, when there is inevitable relational tension between individuals. This begins when people feel misunderstood or not accepted, resulting in them revisiting their wound and pain. Pride can often lead to the need for power or competition which then becomes a threat to the welfare of the wider community.

There is bound to be conflict in any group of people. The skill of building a healthy ecclesial community is recognizing the need to be able to live and work with difference. This must begin with love, and the ability to let go of the need for control, success, to be right or win an argument. Communication difficulties and not listening are usually part of the problem, as people begin to demonize the other and become self-defensive in social interaction. Humility, powerlessness and the centrality of love at the heart of the community need to be the focus, where individuals are encouraged to see the skills and benefits that the other brings to the community.

The formalized virtues and spiritual practices become the bedrock for developing trusting and accepting relationships in the ecclesial community. Some new monastic communities encourage people who have to work hard at maintaining a healthy relationship, meeting regularly to ensure that communication difficulties or problems do not occur or escalate over time. Fear is often part of relational difficulties. Fear is a potent force of our common humanity, and often we do not like people because they touch the parts of our shadow or inner selves that we do not like, which again touches our inner wound enabling resentment and anger to grow.

If communities are to grow through this important stage, individuals within them need to discover the fruits that can be gained by being part of a diverse spiritual community, where people have different views, needs and sensibilities. If love and acceptance can be at the heart of community, it can help people to grow in their common humanity which can be very difficult where there are relational tensions. Where people endure and build trust, then such communities can become transformative, as people then do not need their communities to be uniform and, instead, diversity and imperfection can be celebrated. As Jean Vanier has said:

> The sense of belonging flows from trust: trust is the gradual acceptance of others as they are with their gifts and their limits, each one with the call of Jesus. And this leads to the realization that the body of community is not perfectly whole and cannot be, that this is our human condition. And it is all right for us to be less than perfect. We must not weep over our imperfections. We are not judged for being defective. Our God knows that in many ways we are lame and half-blind ... but we can walk together in hope, celebrating that we are loved in our brokenness.[5]

Our collective spiritual journeys are more accurately seen as a life-long form of discipleship where we quite literally are 'stumbling towards salvation'. If we take any encouragement from the very ordinary disciples in the stories in the Gospels, it is that they spent most of the time being nonplussed, failing and imperfect human beings. However, through their imperfection and endurance, the Christian Church was birthed.

5 Jean Vanier, 1988, *The Broken Body*, London: Darton, Longman and Todd, pp. 98–9.

Once communities are able to live with difference, with a sense of trust and belonging, then they can truly become an open community with those who do not believe. One of the key strategies of new monastic communities is that they give room for people to belong, then to work out if they believe. In a culture where many people are seeking out communities in the hope of finding richly rewarding experience, open forms of community give room for people to encounter God through relationships and the content of shared life. This is what St Francis of Assisi addresses when he reportedly said, 'Preach the Gospel, and when you need to, use words.' So instead of the traditional view of *faith leading to understanding*, this form of community allows people to have *experiences of God that we hope will lead to faith*.

It is an approach to mission and evangelism that assumes that people will experience God to be true through daily life rather than more propositional approaches focused on knowing facts about God. This requires a strong ecclesial community to allow people to 'belong' and to receive, without necessarily contributing very much to the community for a while. This is the missional DNA at the heart of the new monastic model of church. Building such communities is tough, but the rewards once established are substantial.

Community is the outworking of relationships of the heart, seeking to accept people as they are, where no one is seeking to create dependency or power over others. Love gives life, recognizing that all people are beautiful and have value. When people feel loved and trusted, this can often lead people to want to change and grow into becoming more Christlike and therefore more fully human, facing their wounds and developing a world view that is less self-centred or narcissistic. At the same time, community should not be idealized; it is a long, hard journey of becoming who you are and finding unity and holistic wholeness in yourself. In a culture that tells us our identity is found in competition, power, success and wealth, living this way can cost as it is truly countercultural. The emphasis therefore is not on competition but on relating, honouring those around us, where weakness, not strength, becomes the 'cement of our bonding'.[6] The ability

---

6 Vanier, http://speakingoffaith.publicradio.org/programs/wisdomoftenderness/.

to be weak and vulnerable enables us truly to be able to come together and be community, in love, acceptance and trust – and in encounter with the love of God. Otherwise, our fears would crush both us and community, as fear would lead to resentment and aggression.

Living in community requires us to face our prejudices. Prejudice is about prejudging people. Homeless people, severely disabled people and a whole host of others can cause us to unconsciously react in prejudging people as we are driven by fear of the other or unknown. New monastic ecclesial communities follow Jesus Christ, who consciously did not prejudge anyone, but actively loved those who were marginalized and not accepted. We have a lot to learn from the Master. Facing this prejudice in ourselves is the starting place for becoming loving with those in our communities and those who are outside or potentially threatening. This way challenges head-on our prevailing middle-class, consumptive tendencies, and some Christian cultures' emphasis on nuclear relationships over and above the model of ecclesial community as extended families of friends and communities of diversity. Equally, our marriages, boyfriends and girlfriends or our children need not be excuses for not being committed to community. If anything, the lives of married couples, relationships and children can be enriched by being part of such a wide network of people sharing life together as healthy, inclusive life experience over and above the toxic effects of social isolation and the nuclear family.

By establishing trust and belonging, the ecclesial community can become a transformative place of healing from a place that had started with pain. By being committed to weakness and vulnerability, individuals break down the barriers around their hearts about whom they like and don't like, or the excuses of non-engagement, that terrible reality of elitism. By living this way, we encounter the Christ who was the most vulnerable and weak of people, who seeks us to live this way because of God's unconditional love for us, and the mission of God to restore all matter and all creation into restored relationship with the divine.

Forgiveness

Once love, pain, trust and belonging are established, then the place of forgiveness becomes crucial to maintain the depth of community. Without the practice of forgiveness we will go back to the politics of our inner wound and pain resulting in the need for power, self-defensiveness and the need to win arguments to justify the self. If a deep community is to be created and maintained, we need an ongoing powerlessness, vulnerability and love, so forgiveness and humility are crucial virtues that require daily practice.

Forgiveness is the choice to let go, to rise above the need to control or be right, and to choose approaches centred on meditation and finding the common good. Again Jean Vanier names this well:

> Forgiveness is the source and the rock of those who share their lives: to forgive each day, to forgive and forgive and forgive, and to be forgiven just as many times ... Forgiveness is the cement that bonds us together: it is the source of unity; it is the quality of love; that draws together separation ... Forgiveness is letting go of unrealistic expectations of others and of the desire that they be other than they are. Forgiveness is liberating others to be themselves, not making them feel guilty for what may have been ... Forgiveness is to follow Jesus, to be like him, for he came to give and forgive, to take from the shoulders of people the yoke of guilt that locks them into a prison of sadness and sterility, and prevents them from flowing and living freely.[7]

This form of loving forgiveness is one of the greatest gifts of the Christian faith to the world. In a world that is overly punitive, it is both deeply restorative and redemptive. However, it is extremely difficult to live this way. We can only sustain it if we have a deeply resourcing spiritual life. Many of the great heroes of the church – Martin Luther King Jr, Francis of Assisi, Dietrich Bonhoeffer, Teresa of Ávila, Benedict and Desmond Tutu – spent daily time

---

7 Vanier, *Broken*, pp. 106–7.

in prayer. Desmond Tutu when asked by a television journalist whether he had time to pray answered, 'I am too busy to pray for anything less than two hours a day.' To be able to live in such a humble, non-egotistical way requires deep immersion in the love of God, because this way of living costs greatly, and cannot be sustained by the human will alone.

If forgiveness is not at the heart of the community, then deep community cannot be maintained, and communication will become indirect and manipulative. In my experience, communities that have initially established trust, belonging and love sometimes fail because of division created by a lack of forgiveness. So communities need mediators and good pastors to help people find fair settlements between themselves, and where a lack of gentleness, care and love will be challenged. Ultimately, a lack of forgiveness will pollute the heart of the person who is unforgiving, where the pain of their wound becomes enraged in self-defensive justification that seeks retribution and power rather than peace and resolution. This anger may be dressed up in the language of 'justice' or 'righteous anger', but this is effectively a mask for the need to be 'right' and have power over somebody because of an incident or mistake, where the individual takes on the behaviour of an aggrieved victim.

Real justice is more about finding a mediated, just and loving settlement, where those in question remain committed to love, weakness and humility. Some feel that they should not need to talk about problems like this, and the other should just 'get it'. This form of expectation is avoidance, and this effectively compounds problems. Honest communication and feedback are crucial elements of being community.

Within the monastic tradition is the ancient ministry of reconciliation, where the active practice of forgiveness became a focus for discipleship and community life. Holding short accounts with one another, then, is crucial to the health and welfare of a growing community. In some new monastic communities, participants receive formalized communal feedback about how they are progressing regarding their interpersonal development and discipleship. Although this might feel somewhat scary, I can see the merits of a communal approach done in an affirming and loving way, assisting people to develop the practice of forgiveness.

Hope

So when the ecclesial community is able to embed practices of love, openness, belonging and forgiveness, it becomes a truly transformative and hopeful place. There may be only moments when it feels like this, but in so doing it becomes an imperfect visible representation of the invisible, 'now but not fully yet' kingdom of God. Hope is a rare commodity in our modern world, and one that needs work to be maintained:

> Helping each other, growing in trust, living in thanksgiving, learning to forgive, opening up to others, welcoming them, and striving to bring peace and hope to our world. So it is that we come to put down roots in community – not because it is perfect and wonderful, but because we believe that Jesus called us together. It is where we belong and are called to grow and to serve.[8]

When looking to the future, many people are filled with fear as our existence is constantly fragile. We are born and end in weakness and fragility, so many either fear or pin their hopes onto achievement and wealth. Hope then is birthed in the very real experience of the love of God expressed and lived in the life of those choosing to be an ecclesial community. Participating in such a community is an act of hope giving. So we arrive at Christ's teachings encapsulated in the Beatitudes, a profound statement of hope living by the values of the kingdom of God as the basis to ecclesial community:

> Blessed are the poor in spirit, for theirs is the kingdom of heaven. Blessed are those who mourn, for they will be comforted. Blessed are the meek, for they will inherit the earth.

8 Vanier, *Broken*, pp. 99.

Blessed are those who hunger and thirst for righteousness, for they will be filled. Blessed are the merciful, for they will receive mercy. Blessed are the pure in heart, for they will see God. Blessed are the peacemakers, for they will be called children of God. Blessed are those who are persecuted for righteousness' sake, for theirs is the kingdom of heaven. Blessed are you when people revile you and persecute you and utter all kinds of evil against you falsely on my account. Rejoice and be glad, for your reward is great in heaven, for in the same way they persecuted the prophets who were before you. (Matthew 5.3–12)

From what we have witnessed new monastics are able to do this, because they have found inner freedom through the practice of virtues and spiritual disciplines that bring a deeply held sense of peace and hope. The love of God gives members of the community the capacity to act and love others, assisting people to become more fully themselves.

Justice

Once a deep sense of community is established, it can become a challenging metaphor to the world. Since its emerging out of the disciples, the beauty of the Church is that its mission of love, restoration and community has been focused on an upside-down kingdom, focused on the poor and marginalized, following Jesus who came as a weak and vulnerable human being.

Ecclesial communities, made up of the broken and the marginalized, can bring a restored balance to a world driven by the powerful and privileged. As we explored earlier in this book, this meaning goes to the very heart of the Greek word for church, *ekklesia*, spiritual communities made up of slaves, the poor, the marginalized and the excluded. As Eberhard Arnold, founder of the Bruderhof communities[9] in 1920, has said:

---

9 See, http://en.wikipedia.org/wiki/Bruderhof_Communities.

We must live in community because we take our stand in the spiritual fight on the side of all those who fight for freedom, unity, peace and social justice ... Yet we are not the driving force in this – it is we who have been driven and who must be urged on.[10]

By focusing on justice, the ecclesial community becomes a counter-cultural force, encouraging people to re-imagine what is possible when we place ourselves in God's restorative purposes. Here the Lord's Prayer becomes a way of life: 'your kingdom come, your will be done, on earth as it is in heaven'. For many new monastic communities in the USA, this has meant relocation to abandoned places in cities and the countryside, to serve those who are marginalized or forgotten. This way of living seeks to resist the dominance of power and privilege with simple love and care.

Jean Vanier calls this the struggle to live a pleasurable life focused on justice. Joy and pleasure can be the experience of the fulfilment of desire when seen as completing an activity for others well. Communities then focus on *orthopraxis,* enabling members to offer loving service as an act of pleasureful giving to others, offering love and care. Finally, the ecclesial community can sustain the visible call of Christ to 'love one another as I have loved you. By this may all people know that you are my disciples, if you have love one for another' (John 13.34–35).

In a number of traditional monastic orders, participation in governance is part of being a just community. Some, like the Benedictines, elect those to various vocations such as the abbot or prior. People performing such roles are given room to exercise these vocations, but only where there is a strong understanding of being 'one just and inclusive community'.

New monastics have also drawn on a participative and democratic approach to governance. Being community in this context is also about sharing the difficult task of making just decisions. The Moot community in London has a monthly Community Governance meeting, where all those in the community who have

---

10 Eberhard Arnold, 1995, *We Live in Community*, Rifton, NY: Plough Publishing House, pp. 5, 30.

committed to the rhythm of life are invited to share their opinions and partake in decision-making. As with meditation, participative governance requires interpersonal skills and commitment which are again countercultural. In strongly communitarian forms of churches, accountability structures are crucial, not only to the particular people of a community, but more widely, to diocese, district or denomination, and indeed to other new monastic communities. Therefore, structures and decision-making both need to be transparent, to ensure that healthy forms of governance are established.

Some new monastic communities have struggled with having a 'two-speed' community where governance is restricted to an inner core of those involved in leadership. Such forms of governance can easily impoverish the openness of particular new monastic communities, which need to give an important voice to the marginalized and oppressed who are participants in the community. If structures and discernment processes are not clear and transparent, there is the very real danger that a community will revert to hierarchical and un-inclusive forms of church – the very thing new monastic communities are seeking to be an alternative to. Some consider governance by committee as inefficient. We would argue that open forms of governance encourage deeper ownership and participation in the ecclesial community, and help maintain its health, preventing it from becoming a stale institution. Larger new monastic communities will need to develop structures that allow for specialization, in order to sustain complex organizations, but these should always be light in form and as inclusive as possible.

It is also true, however, that communities requiring people to vote about every single detail can become frustratingly slow to make decisions – this effectively kills the ability of the community to change and respond to differing situations. There needs to be a healthy balance between participation and specialization, where differing groups are empowered to make certain decisions within a governance system that holds the wider community together without creating a hierarchical form of church.

Participating in such a deep and justice-orientated new monastic community therefore requires a number of differing approaches to servant leadership. As we have explored earlier, this servant leadership follows the inspiration of Jesus Christ, who humbly loved and supported his disciples to go deeper into the faith through a powerless yet inspirational approach to leadership. This is in keeping with some of the abbots, priors and other leaders I have met from traditional monastic communities. They have been consistently loving and humble yet having enormous wisdom and authority. Most have a deep calling to inspire and to serve communities. There is therefore a need in new monastic communities for highly skilled pastor-teachers and innovators with good interpersonal skills used in the development of new ecclesial communities. This is a challenge to those called to ordained ministry within various denominations, as I perceive the need increasingly for pioneer priests, pastors and innovators, with a skill-set similar to that of monastic abbots or ordained leaders in Franciscan communities. In an increasingly apostolic context, where people in our local environments are largely not Christian, the skill-set of leaders shifts from being a good pastor to more of a missional abbot.

New monastic communities also need members of the community to share in leadership and the curation of both public forms of worship as well as mission and community events. This shared event leadership is important as a form of turn-taking. In the Moot community, weekly worship services are led by different people who are themselves learning about curation and event leadership as part of their ongoing discipleship and belonging to community.

Some commentators of a more Reformed emerging church sensibility seem to hold on to a false paradigm that we do not need leaders. Yet comments such as these often come from charismatic and envisioned people who are in effect leaders, but where this authority is unset or not transparent. People should rightly want to question hierarchical and power-centred forms of leadership, as these can be anachronistic to the building of new monastic missional communities. What is needed are loving and skilled servant leaders who are able to perform such vocations as a form of function, not of privilege or power. Leaders who have faced their inner selves, their wounds and their needs, and have patterned a spiritual life, can then be true inspirations and guides, fully immersed in the love of God.

Mature expressions of ecclesial community require skilled servant leaders, and communities that are prepared to go deep with God and other people are then able to be vulnerable, to give and share love, to be honest, to trust, to forgive, to belong, to face their pains and wounds, to be humble, and to offer loving service to the world. The ecclesial community then becomes the means by which people can encounter God and grow in spiritual awareness.

Afterword

Monastic movements were and are creations crafted by radical Christian communities of faith in response to the promptings and inspiration of the life of the Triune God expressed in the context of the world. If new monasticism is to serve the mission of God through the Church, as we intend, then retrieval – reconnection to the ancient Church, and renewal – the breaking in of God's future, God's new creation – need to go hand in hand. Perhaps then, we can have 'deep church' – a three-dimensional way of life, rooted in ancient practice and living in anticipation of the future.[1]

However, there has been disquiet and questioning of new monasticism. In some quarters of the wider Church, it has been asked whether new monasticism is an authentic expression of the ongoing tradition of the religious life. For some, there has been a concern that we should not mix up the vocation of a monastic monk with being a mendicant friar. It is our contention that new monasticism is an authentic expression of the ongoing tradition of the Christian religious life, while at the same time bringing a new charism or mixed vocation of monk and friar. Admittedly some new monastics are more monk-like and some are more friar-like and this is totally fine. We have been encouraged and blessed by the wisdom of a number of Franciscans and Benedictines who have prayerfully affirmed that they too see this mixed vocation as authentic.

---

1 Graham Cray, 'Why is New Monasticism Important?' in Graham Cray, Ian Mobsby and Aaron Kennedy, 2010, *New Monasticism as Fresh Expression of Church* (Ancient Faith Future Mission), Norwich: Canterbury Press, p. 10.

In this book we have tried to capture and name something of what this movement is and what it is becoming, to understand its roots and heritage and to identify some of the practices which are at its heart. It is clear to us that new monasticism is not simply an evangelism strategy or a romantic withdrawal from the complexities of twenty-first-century life. The movement has to have both a left and right brain. Thus new monasticism attempts to hold together the spiritual and missional life in the crucible of community. For some new monastic communities the story began with a yearning for a spirituality and prayer life that was deep and sacramental, which reflected the ebb and flow of daily life. In finding a rhythm of prayer and worship they engaged with the heart of God for his creation. For others a passion for change, for justice and mercy, led them to find ways that could sustain a life of activism. In doing so they discovered the richness of contemplative and creative prayer. From many starting points and varied routes, groups and communities have found themselves coming together as a movement. At the core of the movement is the call of Jesus in Luke 10.27, 'Love the Lord your God with all your heart and with all your soul and with all your strength and with all your mind' (deepening our relationship with God, the spiritual life) and, 'Love your neighbour as yourself' (deepening our relationship with each other and those whom we live among, the missional life).

In the UK new monasticism faces an interesting future. In 2012, after over a year of deliberations and refinement, the Church of England's Advisory Council on the relations of Bishops and Religious Communities formulated new guidance to help new monastic communities to discern how to become Anglican Acknowledged Religious Communities. This is an exciting next step, and we hope for those communities with some connection to Anglicanism and the Church of England that this will create support, opportunities and recognition of the contribution of new monastic small missional communities to the local church.

If you consider yourself a new monastic in the UK and beyond, we have set up a social media site to increase communication and co-operation between new monastics – http://new-Monasticism-network.ning.com.

We would like to say thank you to those who have inspired and supported us in our communities, practice and thinking over the years. To the members of Moot and safespace, to the Church of England for creating space for new monasticism to begin to flourish and to the monastic and mendicant communities of the traditional religious life who have been generous in their wisdom and patience. In particular Abbot Stuart Burns of Mucknell Abbey, Brothers Samuel and Damian of the Society of St Francis and Sister Joyce of the Community of Saint Francis. We also want to thank you for travelling with us through this book. We hope it will enable you, in some small way, to grow as a follower of God the Creator, Redeemer and Sustainer, as a passionate lover of God and all creation, as a new monastic Christian for the third millennium.

Appendix

Towards Acknowledgement – Guidelines, expectations and advice for a community seeking Acknowledgement as a religious community in the Church of England[1]

The Council is able to register two types of religious communities. The Recognized communities are those in which the members make vows or promises either of stability, conversion of life and obedience or poverty, chastity and obedience. The members of Recognized communities share in a common life and live together, though not necessarily all in one place and have a Rule and Constitutions which provide for the ordering of the life of the community.

The Acknowledged communities vary in their practice and lifestyle. In most cases the members are dispersed, with opportunities provided for meeting together. In some communities, all the members are single, with a vow of celibacy, while in others members may be single or married. Some members of what is otherwise a dispersed community may have a shared life in one place. A community initially established to minister in a particular place, might consist of married members and their families, as well as single members, with all living together in one house, or in several properties near to one another. There are many possibilities and the Council accepts this fluidity and variety and seeks to encourage this growth in community life in the Church.

---

1 Taken from the leaflet 'Towards Acknowledgement – Guidelines, expectations and advice for a community seeking Acknowledgement as a religious community in the Church of England', unpublished, January 2013.

The distinction between the Recognized and Acknowledged communities is necessary in order to honour the single or unmarried state and the sharing of a common life, which have always been characteristic features of the religious life and also because the professed members of the Recognized communities elect representatives to the General Synod.

The Handbook of the Religious Life, published by Canterbury Press for the Council (available from Church House bookshop), contains much useful information and guidance. Those communities looking at the possibility of Acknowledgement should consult it, bearing in mind that some of the detailed provision is provided mainly for the Recognized communities.

Both Recognized and Acknowledged communities can be ecumenical in their membership. In the case of an Acknowledged community this would need to be reflected in its governance documents and in those chosen as episcopal (or equivalent) sponsors. When appointing a Visitor, the community would probably need to have two or three people to exercise this ministry jointly. The Council would expect one of them to be an Anglican bishop.

Process for Acknowledgement

Communities that seek Acknowledgement vary considerably in size, gifts and focus of ministry. It is not possible to establish a detailed procedure that fits all of them. The intention of the Council in providing a process is to enable a community which is considering Acknowledgement to discern the leading of the Holy Spirit in its life. This process is not intended to be a series of hoops to jump through, hurdles to be jumped, boxes to be ticked or any other appropriate metaphor. The Council seeks to provide support and encouragement. The process that is outlined and the guidelines that are provided are intended to help a community give attention to key aspects of its life.

It is not necessary for a community which is considering Acknowledgement to wait until it feels it might be ready for Acknowledgement before making contact with the Council. The

Council encourages communities to contact the Council in the early stages of the community's life. The best way to do this is for the leader or a person appointed by the community to contact the Chairman of the Council. Once the information that the Council needs has been gathered, the Council will appoint one or two members to liaise with the community, to provide advice and support and to ensure that the contact between the community and the Council is maintained.

During this time the Council will expect the community to look at the following areas of its life. Some of these things the community may well have already worked on, others will need clarification and others will be new. All of them will need to have reached a satisfactory stage for the community to be considered for Acknowledgement.

Guidelines and expectations

1. The community needs to be able to say what its particular vocation is in the service of the gospel. It should be able to express how it feels God has called it into being and what gifts he is giving for its life and ministry.
2. There needs to be a Rhythm or Rule of Life which seeks to express the particular aspirations and practices of the community. This does not need to be a very detailed document and needs to be flexible to leave room for development.
3. It is important that the community seeks ways for its particular calling to be formed in the life of its members.
4. The community must draw up guidelines about its expectations of leadership, how the leader is chosen, elected or replaced and the length of time of periods of office. It must do similar things for any leadership group that might be formed and ensure that there are clear accountability structures, where appropriate.
5. The community must ensure it has good structures for governing the life of the community so that the views of each member can be clearly heard. Eventually the community will need to

draw up a constitution or governance document. Chapter 7 of the Handbook provides a useful structure for this and the areas that might need to be covered but initially a community seeking Acknowledgement should keep its governance documents simple.

6. Financial matters must be dealt with carefully and records kept of donations made and expenses paid. How this is done will depend on the size of the community but whatever the method, great care is needed as this is an area in which difficulties and misunderstandings can arise.

7. The community needs to be able to express its involvement and commitment to the life of the Church. This will vary according to the particular vocation of the community. In the case of a dispersed community, for example, this will depend on the particular ministry of each of the members. For a community living a common life in a particular place, it will most likely be expressed in the life of the local church and in the life of the diocese. It is important that a community doesn't see itself as, or develop into, an alternative church.

8. The community needs to develop a working relationship with a bishop, who will act as an episcopal advisor and sponsor. When the members of a community are in several dioceses, the community must find a bishop who is willing to take on this responsibility. When a community is located in one diocese, the initial contact and support should come from the diocesan bishop. In either case, the agreement of the diocesan bishop must be sought for any necessary liturgical authorization.

9. The members of the community must not make vows or promises without the agreement of the Council. It is not necessary for a community to be Acknowledged before agreement for vows to be taken will be given but the Council will not agree that life vows or promises can be made until the community is Acknowledged.

10. There will need to be at least six members of the community before Acknowledgement will be given.

Acknowledgement

When the community decides that it wishes to seek for Acknowledgement by the Council and the member or members of the Council who are advising the community support this, then the procedure could be as follows.

1. The leader or leadership team of the Community should ask the diocesan or sponsoring bishop to write to the Chairman of the Council, formally requesting Acknowledgement.
2. The community should be able to present to the Council a Rule or Rhythm of Life and governance documents or constitutions in accordance with the guidance given.
3. If not already done, an Episcopal Visitor will need to be appointed.
4. It is envisaged that the community and the member or members of the Council acting as advisors will have worked together to ensure that everything has been done to comply with the guidelines for Acknowledgement laid down by the Council. The Council may ask for further clarification of certain matters if it sees fit.
5. If the Council agrees with the request for Acknowledgement, the secretary of the Council writes to the diocesan or sponsoring bishop, the leader of the community and the Visitor to inform them.
6. The secretary of the Council enters the community in the register of Acknowledged Communities.
7. The secretary of the Council writes to the editor of Anglican Religious Life to ask for the community to be included in the next edition.
8. It is hoped that the process would conclude with an appropriate commissioning service.

Resources

Below are a number of resources that we hope will assist you.

Websites

New Monasticism Network	http://new-Monasticism-network.ning.com
Fresh Expressions	http://www.freshexpressions.org.uk
Anglican religious communities	http://communities.anglicancommunion.org/
New Monasticism USA	http://www.newMonasticism.org
24-7 Community	http://uk.24-7prayer.com
Moot	http://www.moot.uk.net
safespace	http://www.freshexpressions.org.uk/stories/safespace
Northumbria Community	http://www.northumbriacommunity.org
Church of the Apostles	http://www.apostleschurch.org
Contemplative Fire	http://www.contemplativefire.org
maybe	http://maybe.org.uk

Books

Ian Adams (2010) *Cave Refectory Road: Monastic Rhythms for Contemporary Living*, Norwich: Canterbury Press.

Ian Adams (2013) *Running Over Rocks: Spiritual Practices to Transform Tough Times*, Norwich: Canterbury Press.

Shane Claiborne (2006*) Irresistible Revolution: Living as an Ordinary Radical*, Grand Rapids, MI: Zondervan.

Graham Cray, Ian Mobsby and Aaron Kennedy (2010) *New Monasticism as Fresh Expression of Church* (Ancient Faith, Future Mission), Norwich: Canterbury Press.

Simon Cross (2010) *Totally Devoted: The Challenge of New Monasticism*, Franklin, TN: Authentic Publications.

Peta Dunstan (2011) *Anglican Religious Life 2014–15: A Yearbook of Religious Orders and Communities in the Anglican Communion*, Norwich: Canterbury Press.

Andy Freeman and Pete Greig (2007) *Punk Monk: New monasticism and the Ancient Art of Breathing*, Eastbourne: Kingsway Publications.

Ian Mobsby (2012) *God Unknown: The Trinity in Contemporary Spirituality and Mission*, Norwich: Canterbury Press.

Ray Simpson (1995) *Exploring Celtic Spirituality: Historic Roots for Our Future*, London: Hodder & Stoughton Religious.

The Advisory Council (2004) *A Handbook of Religious Life*, Norwich: Canterbury Press.

Jonathan Wilson-Hartgrove (2008) *New Monasticism: What It Has to Say to Today's Church*, Ada, MI: Brazos Press.